One of *The London Times'* Be[...]
Autostraddle's Best LGB[...]
Book Riot's Best Queer Books of 20[...]
BuzzFeed's Best Nonfiction of 2018,
Out's Best Queer Books of 2018, and
The Saturday Paper's Best Books of 2018

"In an age when identity feels so splintered and fractional, McBee's empathy with men feels refreshing, but it's his determination to be accountable that is radical. He resolves his own masculinity crisis by doing the things men often think they're doing, but so often are not: listening, asking questions, seeking help, being vulnerable."

—*The Guardian*

"This book relays a subtle, profound personal investigation into masculinity and personhood. . . . McBee's great twist is to treat masculinity itself as an anthropological phenomenon, represented by this bloody, extreme sport. Inside the fight, McBee finds reconciliation."

—*The New Republic*

"A no-holds-barred examination of masculinity. McBee describes the journey as a way of grappling with his newish place in the world of toxic (and privileged) masculinity. . . . A compassionate look at what it means to be a man and the circumstances that have engendered our expectations. It is in many ways a happy dismantling of these expectations, an opening of masculinity to make room for love, support, and tenderness— something McBee is pleasantly surprised to find along the way."

—*BuzzFeed*

"Thomas Page McBee's new memoir, *Amateur*, is a powerful exploration of the costs of toxic masculinity and the joys of an authentic life. It is also a classic fight story. Superbly written and keenly observed, *Amateur* manages to juggle all of these elements with grace and wit."

—*The Rumpus*

"McBee is consistently vulnerable—both physically and in how he shares his experience. Yet at the end of *Amateur*, after all the punches, interviews, and introspection, the author does not arrive at any simple answers. Instead, that initial question about men and fighting multiplies into larger ones. . . . While he gets closer and closer to that eventual fight night in New York, his investigation of men is made more powerful by this lack of certainty—ultimately asking whether anyone, including those who flaunt their political strength in Washington, DC, truly comprehends the meaning of masculinity."

—*Bitch* magazine

"It is no coincidence that the terms 'masculinity crisis' and 'toxic masculinity' have become current at a time when leaders such as presidents Putin and Trump strut the world stage like parodies of the archetypal alpha male. Who better to explore this crisis than someone who has had to interrogate, with every cell of their body, what it means to become a man? . . . With exhilarating clarity and tenderness, *Amateur* exposes patriarchy for the construct that it is."

—*The Sydney Morning Herald*

"[McBee's] writing asks questions about gender that he believes are relevant to all people, trans or not. . . . [*Amateur*] probes the culture (or cult) of masculinity through, among other things, his experience as the first trans man to enter the boxing ring at Madison Square Garden, where he competed in a 2015 charity event when he was thirty-four."

—*Newsday*

"Elegantly demonstrate[s] how men can fight for a better definition of manhood—one that includes vulnerability, empathy, and self-expression—simply by fighting to be themselves . . . [McBee] finds the answer not in knocking out another man's mouthguard, but rather in moments of vulnerability and the nurturing gestures of other men."

—*Quartz*

"Using as a springboard his experiences training to fight in a charity boxing match, McBee untangles the troublesome relationship between masculinity and violence. From his perspective as a trans man, he tackles the limitations of conventional masculinity, and maps a path forward to a new kind of masculinity."

—Autostraddle

"The hot center of this book, the new work that it does, is McBee's search to identify and adopt ways to be a 'better' man. He wants to know, as a man, how to fight gender inequity. . . . At a time when equity of all kinds is being suppressed, *Amateur* is a reminder that the individual can still come forward and fight."

—The A.V. Club

"*Amateur* is Thomas Page McBee's poetic exploration of (sometimes toxic) masculinity as he trained to become the first trans man to box in Madison Square Garden. Author of the award-winning memoir *Man Alive*, McBee expected men drawn to boxing were motivated by bloodlust. Instead, he discovers mentorship among men overcoming weaknesses. In finding the vulnerability guys hope to hide, McBee finds hope for all men."

—The Advocate

"McBee ruminates on his own insecurity about his masculinity, on the masculinity crisis in the US, and has conversations with his siblings about the own experiences with masculinity. I loved how self-reflective McBee is, such as when he realized, after the fact, that he and his brother had cut out their sister's voice. He immediately apologized, and won a place in my heart as a genuinely kind man who just wanted to learn to punch people in the face. This is a book I'll definitely return to again."

—Book Riot

"McBee takes a hard look at masculinity and its effects on him as a trans man, as he prepares for a charity boxing match, having had no previous ring training. The result is a short but powerful glimpse into a man who, despite his muscles and beard, fears that his hard-won masculinity is leading him down a rougher path than he anticipated. . . . Gritty and lyrical . . . Using copious research as well as his own experiences, McBee delivers a knockout punch of gender and societal rumination, paralleled with his own journey as a boxer. . . . *Amateur* is a unique and self-aware take on masculinity, its problems, and its potential. McBee's voice is as strong as his presence in the ring, and his willingness to pick apart his newfound privilege is a positive example for all men. *Amateur* is a deft peek into the inner life of one who has already transitioned to his true gender, and is now coming to terms with what that means."

—*Windy City Times*

"Candid and conversational . . . a memoir of trans identity that's also a complicated exploration of modern day masculinity and the gender roles that all of us play . . . it's compelling as hell to read."

—*Salon*

"McBee has honed his writing to the meet the task of taking readers deep inside his experience, fearful only of stereotypes, superficialities, and clichés. It asks as much of the reader's integrity—reading without presumptions, without reading in—as it does of the author's. . . . Even with the author's interjecting questions about his development and changing character, his story of getting to Madison Square Garden—both within and on the ropes—for a charity match moves right along. But it's his constantly shifting, occasionally feinting, always deepening reflections on the porous boundaries between aggression and violence, the fighter and the fought, masculinity as taught and susceptible of being relearned, that sometimes make you forget he's on his way to win or lose or both or neither in the glare and roar of the Garden. . . . The experience he reveals is at once unwaveringly personal and enlivened by the insights he, as a trained journalist-writer, has gained by interviewing the experts on gender, sexuality, and masculinity."

—*Bay Area Reporter*

"Thomas Page McBee is a trans man who opts to train as a boxer in order to fight in a charity match. The training sends him into uncomfortable territory as he works to unpack whether violence is a necessary component of the maleness to which he has transitioned. He provides readers with a fascinating, poignant account of his desire to push at the constructions of what it means to be a man in order to better understand himself."

—*Signature Reads*

"This is an extraordinary, humane, and compassionate book about aggression, selfhood, and love. Nothing short of superb."

—*Attitude*

"When men fight, they are fighting the parts of themselves they hate, as McBee, himself a victim of abuse, discovers . . . [the account] is interspersed with insights from a wide range of commentators and experts on issues relating to masculinity, race, gender, and violence. It all adds up to a gripping and fascinating journey."

—Press Association

"In this memoir from Scribner, [McBee] grapples with masculinity, gender, and violence as he recounts his training to become a boxer."

—*The Writer*

"Reading *Amateur* is watching someone try to simultaneously figure out who they are, who the world wants them to be, and why. It's deeply personal and politically vital, a calm and contemplative antidote to male toxicity."

—*The Skinny*

"Sharp and precise, open and honest . . . It's hard to overstate how important and profound it feels to read a personal account of a man actively examining his own masculinity and privilege in such an honest way."

—*Women's Review of Books*

"[McBee's] writing is marvelous, pinning ideas that could so easily be abstract to the visceral, physical poetry of boxing. . . . McBee displays tenacity on the page and in the gym, sizing up formidable concepts and engaging them with savvy and sensitivity. *Amateur* is more than a boxing story, just as it's more than a trans narrative. It's a highly recommended case study in manhood."

—*Shelf Awareness*

"This powerful book chronicles McBee's training and his attempts at understanding why violence is accepted as an aspect of American masculinity. . . . McBee's lyrical, achingly honest exploration of loss and maturation offers a hopeful antidote to more toxic forms of masculinity."

—*Publishers Weekly* (starred review)

"Riveting. [McBee] is a compelling narrator. A heartfelt glimpse of a trans person's life, with a very dramatic boxing match bringing into focus the gender binary . . . Readers will be able to relate and gain new perspectives."

—*Library Journal*

"This timely memoir explores male-female power dynamics in an uplifting story of someone who becomes a new man in ways even he couldn't anticipate."

—*Booklist*

"In this lyrical, courageous book, the author eloquently probes his inner life as he searches for the meaning of gender identity in a world limited by binary thinking. Provocative and illuminating—a winning follow-up to McBee's acclaimed debut."

—*Kirkus Reviews*

"Until I read this book, I didn't realize how tired I was of reading about masculinity as cold, hard, and fixed. *Amateur* is a warm hug. It's also an invitation to everyone who's ever struggled to accept failure, searched for a sense of belonging, or said '*Ugh, men*' in an exasperated tone to think harder and be kinder. I want the world to read it."

—Ann Friedman, *New York* magazine columnist and cohost of *Call Your Girlfriend*

"*Amateur* is a brutally honest look at the problems with masculinity, laced through with hope and joy and possibility. Thomas McBee confronts fears and realities with grace, toughness, and poetry. A beautiful book."

—Michelle Tea, author of *Black Wave* and *How to Grow Up*

"Thomas Page McBee's *Amateur* takes a classic, well-worn subject—a man whose fight with other men is ultimately a confrontation with the self—and completely revitalizes, renews, and enriches it. McBee grapples with enormous issues such as masculinity, identity, transformation, and loss with great depth and intelligence, and in doing so, explores so many of the tough questions we should all be asking ourselves. Though slim and sharply concise, *Amateur* enlarges the world by opening up greater, more hopeful realms of possibility. I am a better man for having read this book."

—Isaac Fitzgerald, founding editor of BuzzFeed Books, cohost of *#AMtoDM*, and coauthor of *Pen & Ink* and *Knives & Ink*

"Thomas Page McBee is a fighter—and not only in a ring in Madison Square Garden. *Amateur* shows us a warrior of the human spirit, courageously investigating masculinity itself. His prose—both fierce and delicate—reveals a struggle to become a better man, and to create a better self. *Amateur* is urgent, generous, and fearless."

—Jennifer Finney Boylan, author of *Long Black Veil* and *She's Not There*

"With Thomas as your gloved guide, you'll peer into locker rooms, through ropes, and at douchebags challenging strangers to sidewalk beatdowns. Watch Thomas spar with masculinity as he takes on his, your, and America's manhood. While tracing his journey from uninitiated fighter to Madison Square Garden boxer, McBee explores why men so frequently confuse violence with power and why being a man ought to rely on a willingness to spar, first and foremost, with one's own shadow."

—Myriam Gurba, author of *Mean*

"A blazingly wise and beautiful book."

—A. L. Kennedy, author of *All the Rage* and *Serious Sweet*

"*Amateur* provocatively describes the ways in which an increasingly fragile patriarchal culture needs to keep men in their place. A quest for self-liberation, this loving and deeply intelligent exploration of contemporary masculinities is essential reading."

—Deborah Levy, author of *Swimming Home* and *Hot Milk*

Also by Thomas Page McBee

Man Alive: A True Story of Violence,
Forgiveness and Becoming a Man

AMATEUR

RECKONING WITH GENDER,
IDENTITY, AND MASCULINITY

Thomas Page McBee

SCRIBNER
New York   London   Toronto   Sydney   New Delhi

Scribner
An Imprint of Simon & Schuster, Inc.
1230 Avenue of the Americas
New York, NY 10020

First Scribner trade paperback edition May 2019

This book was previously published with the subtitle
A True Story About What Makes a Man.

For information about special discounts for bulk purchases,
please contact Simon & Schuster Special Sales at 1-866-506-1949
or business@simonandschuster.com.

The Simon & Schuster Speakers Bureau can bring authors to your live event.
For more information or to book an event, contact the Simon & Schuster Speakers
Bureau at 1-866-248-3049 or visit our website at www.simonspeakers.com.

Interior design by Erich Hobbing

Manufactured in the United States of America

5   7   9   10   8   6

Library of Congress Cataloging-in-Publication Data

Names: McBee, Thomas Page, author.
Title: Amateur : a true story about what makes a man /
Thomas Page McBee.
Description: New York : Scribner, 2018.
Identifiers: LCCN 2017061731 | ISBN 9781501168741 (hardback) |
ISBN 9781501168758 (tp) | ISBN 9781501168765 (eISBN)
Subjects: LCSH: Men—Identity. | Masculinity—Social aspects. |
Men—Psychology. | BISAC: SOCIAL SCIENCE / Gender
Studies. | SOCIAL SCIENCE / Men's Studies. |
BIOGRAPHY & AUTOBIOGRAPHY / General.
Classification: LCC HQ1090 .M394 2018 | DDC 155.3/32—dc23
LC record available at https://lccn.loc.gov/2017061731

ISBN 978-1-5011-6874-1
ISBN 978-1-5011-6875-8 (pbk)
ISBN 978-1-5011-6876-5 (ebook)

For my mom,
Carol Lee McBee,
who taught me how to fight

In the beginner's mind there are many possibilities, but in the expert's there are few.

—Shunryu Suzuki,
Zen Mind, Beginner's Mind

Me: "I wish you could experience how differently people react to me now that I'm a man."
My brother: "I can't imagine, but I can imagine."

AMATEUR

November 2015

According to the laws of physics and USA Boxing, this wasn't a fair fight. But there we were, two guys past our primes, circling each other in front of seventeen hundred drunk onlookers in Madison Square Garden, that hallowed hall of American boxing.

Since July, I'd bled at the gums and screamed into pillows and almost quit. I'd failed. I'd temporarily, and to varying degrees, lost my mind, my hearing, and my friends. All so that a guy with seventeen pounds on me could beat bruises across my face, both of us a messy mosaic of blurred senses, damp armpits, hot lights, tangy throat, rubber-mouthguard bite marks, squeaky pivots, spangles of stars.

All so that my fists could connect with his stomach, and his mine. It would hurt, the stinging price of knowing my body's upper limits, but for now my muscles harmonized out their combinations as a meditative quiet sucked the cheers out of the stadium. I understood that we were both just sinew, and blood, and bone, and follicles, and decay.

The truth was, I loved him even as I danced around him with my hands in the air. I was a new man, the first transgender man to fight in the most storied boxing venue on earth, there to close the gap between us like the fiction that it is.

Why Am I Doing This?

Why do men fight? What makes some of us want to get hit in the face? What makes others show up to watch?

What makes a man?

When I first began injecting testosterone, I was thirty years old and needed to become beautiful to myself. I clocked my becoming primarily in aesthetic terms: the T-shirt that now fit me, the graceful curl of a biceps, the glorious sprinkle of a beard. I loved the way men looked, and smelled, and held themselves. I loved their lank and bulk and ease, their straight-razor barbershop shaves, their chest-first centers of balance. I loved the quiet efficiency of the men's restroom, the ineffable physical joy of running alongside my brother, the shadows we cut against the buildings we passed.

I loved being a man in that I loved having a body.

I had surgery to reconstruct my chest; I stuck a long needle into the meat of my thigh each week; I changed my name and my place in the world—all so I could quit hiding behind pulled-low baseball hats and rash guards, free to pull off my shirt and jump right into the waves.

The joys I found at first were daily, simple, and rooted in the warm physicality of a new freedom—toweling off after a shower and catching a glimpse of my flat chest in a foggy mirror; the way clothes suddenly fit my squarer shoulders and slimmer hips. The extra muscle mass that squared my walk, broadened my hands, my calves, my throat. I touched the dip of my abs, half-naked in the bathroom, and the muscle and skin synced in the mirror. I turned, and he turned. I smiled, and he smiled. I expanded, and so did he.

Stories about trans people, when we hear them at all, often end with such shining symbolism, meant to indicate that the man or woman in question has succeeded, in the transition, in the grand task of *finally being themselves*. Though that's lovely, and even a little true, in the same way a pregnancy or a near-death experience can act on the body like gravity, reshaping our days and memories and even time around its impact—it isn't where my story ends. Not even close.

I am a beginner, a man born at thirty, with a body that reveals a reality about being human that is rarely examined. Most of us experience gender conditioning so young—research shows it begins in infancy—that we misunderstand the relationship between nature and nurture, culture and biology, fitting in and *being oneself*.

This book is an attempt to pull apart those strands. It also became, as I wrote it, a kind of personal insurance, a way to track and shape my own becoming in a culture where so many men are poisonous.

I too come from a long line of poisonous men.

• • •

As the testosterone took hold and reshaped my body, its impact as an object in space grew increasingly bewildering: the expectation that I not be afraid juxtaposed against the fear I inspired in a woman, alone on a dark street; the silencing effect of my voice in a meeting; the unearned presumption of my competence; my power; my potential.

I could feel myself forming in response to conference calls and tollbooth workers and first dates. I was like a plant in the sun, moving toward whatever was rewarded in me: aggression, ambition, fearlessness.

So I shrugged into men's T-shirts, which suddenly and beautifully fit, trying to pretend that I wasn't stuck between stations, the static giving way to errant pieces of concerning advice I picked up along the way, a mounting dissonance I pushed aside until an otherwise ordinary spring day when the troubling gap between my past life and my new body could no longer be ignored.

• • •

To the strangers nearby on Orchard Street, the scene must have seemed innocuous. I looked like any other Lower East Side white guy in his thirties: tattooed, skinny, in sneakers and sunglasses. But I was just four years on testosterone. My beard, complete with errant gray hairs, telegraphed a life I hadn't yet fully lived.

Plus, my guard was down. I'd just left Jess, my new girlfriend, upstairs in my apartment, the promise of an empty evening spread out before us, and I was on my way to the bodega for ice cream when I clocked that the new restaurant with the beautiful front window had finally opened up next door. With a learned confidence I texted, "I'm taking you here tonight," alongside a photo I snapped of the "modern British" spot, capturing—in the glary bounce of my accidental flash—its impossibly cool new denizens, framed by that window in a soft and romantic light.

"Hey!" I looked up, catching the gooey spring light through the trees like a breath before going under, knowing, in the way of animals, that I'd surrendered my night to the big-bicepsed guy in a white T-shirt coming my way. "Are you taking a picture of my fucking car, man?" he shouted, his voice strangely hoarse.

I studied his approach, the moment expanding already into something bigger, people dumbly moving out of the way, gawking but not interfering. This was the third near scuffle I'd found myself in, in as many months. It was otherworldly the way an otherwise-idyllic moment could suddenly tip toward violence. As he came into focus, I locked up with dread.

A queasy fear wavered through me.

The Before me wanted to run, as I had run from my stepfather as a child, this stranger and the man who'd raised me sharing, momentarily, the same scary, bald menace.

"Hey!" the stranger said. He had dark, wavy hair and a blurry mass of tattoos on his forearm, and the unkempt look of the newly divorced. He seemed drunk.

I intuited that he wanted attention, that he hoped to not only cause a scene, but to leave the exchange with black-eyed proof of it.

Men don't run. The unwanted thought appeared in my brain, through the static.

And so I heaved a great sigh and turned toward him because that's what men do. I asked him in the lowest tone I could rumble "What in the fuck" he wanted. He pointed at a bright red Mercedes parked in front of the restaurant—the kind of car that looked like a dick. Sweat clung to his face, too much for the chilly afternoon. I took in the wildness in his eyes and was surprised to feel both scared of and sorry for him. What would Mom say? *Keep it in perspective.* The voice was so precisely hers, it was as if she were really next to me. *Thomas,* she warned me, when I balled my fists.

He looked haunted, I thought, relaxing my hands.

"I was taking a photo of the restaurant in front of your car," I tried, softening my tone a bit, breaking the rules of the scene. "I want to take my girlfriend on a date there." I remembered, at the last moment, not to add an upward lilt to the end of my thought.

"I saw the flash!" he growled, beyond logic, a man committed to his part.

That was the worst of it, I realized. He couldn't even see me.

I could be anyone.

● ● ●

"Men don't hug," my uncle told me, extending his hand on a warm day a few years before. It was offered kindly, my new life a stream of unsolicited advice, a guide to the construction of a passable masculinity.

He wasn't wrong. Jess was often the only person who touched me. It struck me that this unfriendly, unshaven man before me now needed human contact.

I too knew what it was like to be near-mad with that sort of need. I may have learned through dumb practice to walk with my chest out, just as I'd trained myself to

8

limit exclamation points in my correspondence, but I felt all the absences my male body created too: the cool distance of friends in tough moments, stemming to some degree from the self-conscious way I held myself apart from women especially, so concerned with being perceived as a threat that I'd become a ghost instead. I'd accepted these prices of admission at first, but lately every day felt like a struggle against a bad translation. What had happened to me?

Done with the charade, I turned away from the angry stranger on Orchard Street, but he clotheslined me as I attempted to move on, his meaty arm stretching out across the length of my chest scars, matching with odd precision the reminder of the technology that allowed me this moment, this rich reward of being "in the right body" at last.

I could smell a mint on his breath, and the confirmation of liquor beneath it. It was late afternoon. I looked at him sadly. "Give. Me. Your. Phone," he said, emphasizing each word, as if he sensed my empathy and wanted to destroy it.

He and I both waited for me to do something. But what? He had seventy-five pounds and five inches on me. Was I to hit him? Could I? I studied the dart of his eyes. I could, if I had to.

A base and primal instinct grabbed me as I waited for him to twitch. It felt terrible and good to give into it. I stared at him, calculating the distance between us. He wobbled, and then smiled viciously when I flinched, telegraphing the kind of masculinity that I knew, that I could *smell*, compensated for some deep maw of insecurity. It was hard to tell, as it always is, if he was the kid who got bullied or the bully himself. Still, a part of me wanted to live out that worn masculine narrative of risking my body to prove my right to exist in it.

You are a child of the universe, read the poem my mom had given me in a birthday card long ago, *you have a right to be here.* Grief whistled through my chest. My phone buzzed, disrupting our dark reverie. It was surely Jess, asking after me. I wanted to be upstairs with her, eating ice cream in that narcotic new-love bliss. Why was I down here, making my body a weapon instead?

I was a man, that much was clear. But, years after I became one, I still wondered what, exactly, that meant.

• • •

It wasn't lost on me that others were asking the same question.

The first few years I'd injected testosterone coincided with a period of anxious headlines about men in economic turmoil. Post-recession, a surge in suicides, drug addiction, and even beards were all blamed on a broader insecurity about the massive loss of jobs and the shake-up of male-led households after the crash. It was dubbed a global "masculinity crisis." (This idea, not new in academic circles, now caught fire in popular culture.) In the United States, the story went, men were (sometimes reluctantly) becoming stay-at-home dads, or going back to school in traditionally female-dominated fields such as nursing, or—to avoid doing that—moving back in with their parents and playing video games all day. It was, according to a 2010 cover story in *The Atlantic*, "the end of men."

A certain sort of man—white, rural, older—it seemed, was disappearing, and dying, and killing, and overdosing. These men did seem to be in crisis, in the broadest possible sense. But it did not appear to be the end of the masculinity, at least not to me. From the moment the testosterone kicked in, nearly everyone around me was invested in educating me in how to ape the strong-and-silent stereotype of the man whose reign was "over"—a socialization that involved relentless policing by strangers and friends alike, and across gender, geographic, and socioeconomic lines. Whatever compelled these instructions, they seemed core to manhood itself, and maybe that's why I became obsessed with chronicling the "masculinity crisis"—both the unfolding economic fallout that stemmed from a fundamentalist gender narrative linking masculinity to work, and the way I found its many echoes in my own experience of dislocation in this body. Because of my conditioning, I suspected that the "crisis" was far more complex than people understood, that its root cause was far deeper than class and race and "tradition," that the bedrock of the crisis was inherent in masculinity itself, and therefore it encompassed all men, even the ones who felt they successfully defied outdated conventions. It was, after all, the men who read books on emotional intelligence and wore tailored shirts who often advised me, with the casual, camouflaged sexism of the urbane, to treat dating like warfare, or to dominate meetings with primate body language.

It seemed to me that being in crisis was a natural reaction to being a man, any man, even if that wasn't precisely what anyone else meant.

I started thinking about all of this back in 2011, the year I first injected testosterone. I'd just landed my first full-time journalism job as an editor at a newspaper in Boston, following the headlines with macabre curiosity from the United States to the United Kingdom and eventually as far east as China. In the United States, the story morphed quickly into the now-familiar tale of class and generational stratification: Poorer men were being "left behind" by the rise of education rates for women and the trend away from marriage in lower income brackets.

Meanwhile, well-off "makers" in cities dressed like lumberjacks and dabbled in bespoke artisan crafts to reconnect with old-fashioned, hands-on work, but with attitudes toward masculinity that many men insisted were radically different from previous generations. Millennial guys seemed, to the sociologists and anthropologists who studied them, to have attitudes toward women that portended a new era of equity—especially at work. But the reality was, indeed, far more complicated. Later surveys and studies would suggest that Millennial men as a whole turned out to be as "traditional," and even less egalitarian, in their attitudes toward gender as their fathers—which made experts eventually posit that growing up with fathers impacted by the masculinity crisis made them more, not less, resistant to gender equality.

But that came later. Back in 2013, about a year before that disappointing story began to emerge, I lost my journalism job in Boston to massive layoffs. I was living cheaply enough to subsist on freelance and contract work, so I chose optimism, casting around for story ideas about men who seemed to be using the crisis as an opportunity to challenge the negative aspects of manhood. And they were out there: Men were more engaged fathers, experts said. Rap stars and pro athletes came out. Bromantic comedies about the platonic love between friends beat out traditional, more sexist buddy comedies at the box office. I needed those stories, needed those men, taking solace in the idea that I wasn't the only guy seeking a different answer from the one I'd found in the models that had shaped me, growing up in a small town outside Pittsburgh.

But the more I felt at home in my body, the more my discomfort with what was expected of it deepened. Later that year, I moved to New York and spent most of my free time on terrible first dates I couldn't afford with women I couldn't figure out. I wasn't sure how to tell them I was trans, or if I even should, but I also didn't understand how to transcend the surprising traditionalism that masked our every interaction.

As I struggled to make sense of my place in the world, the economy improved and certain cultural shifts around fatherhood in particular did seem to take hold, but the masculinity crisis raged on. Men I grew up with killed themselves. As an opioid epidemic surged, social media bifurcated Americans. I could see the splinter in my own feeds, where I found a readership for my stories, but trolls tweeted at me in response to nearly everything I wrote. "You're not a man," they said, over and over. "And you never will be."

It was 2015. Everyone told me to "not read the comments," but it all—the policing, the dating, the sexism, the trolls, the Millennials, the opioids, the "makers"—

it all seemed connected. I couldn't shake the idea that this larger masculinity crisis held in its bitter center a truth that reflected something important and terrifying about what we talk about when we talk about men. All men. Something bigger than a generation, or a political moment, or an economic crash—a story about masculinity that we all, every one of us, has been taught to believe.

• • •

"Maybe, instead of looking for the men you want to be, you need to face your worst fears about who you are," Jess said, early in our courtship. She wondered if my notions of masculinity were unrealistically "romantic." I wasn't so sure she was right, but her invitation to examine my fears so terrified me, I tried to avoid thinking about it, until my run-in with the man on Orchard Street clarified her wisdom. There he was, finally, my awful mirror: when he balled his fists, I balled mine. If you happened upon the scene and didn't know me, you'd be hard-pressed to identify what made us so different, and you'd be right.

"Hey!" the man shouted, and that wickedness coursed through me even as I marshaled the self-control to turn and walk away, tracking his ever-louder footfalls, leading him toward Seward Park, where at least there were parents and children playing on the slides,

New Yorkers who, I hoped, would tend to me if I was knocked to my knees in front of them.

Moms, I mean.

"Hey!" he shouted, as we approached the corner, and then, more menacingly, "Asshole!"

A group of roughhousing boys, quieted perhaps by a real-life scene of what they playacted, turned to look.

I was embarrassed. I wanted to be held. I wanted to drink tea in a living room warm with sunlight in a world I could understand. I wanted a life I would never again have. I looked at the man with the sweaty forehead and dusty beard, and I let an acidic rage bloom in the place of all I'd lost, coloring my tone such a ragged mess I didn't recognize my own voice. *"I. Did. Not. Take. A. Picture. Of. Your. Fucking. Car."*

He backed away with his hands up. "Okay, okay," he mumbled. "Jesus."

I leaned against a wall. Something had to change.

• • •

In my corner of New York, the masculinity crisis was increasingly taken for granted—something happening to other men, far away.

"Men keep trying to fight me," I told my friends, my brother, my coworkers after that day on Orchard Street. Most people shrugged. *Weird,* they said. What could you do?

16

It was 2015, when I began this book, and we were looking toward the future. When I said I was writing about masculinity, people didn't react as they did at the start of the crisis—more and more, they smiled politely and changed the subject. I understood. A lot of people felt as if we had been talking about a certain kind of man for long enough. It was easier to believe that we lived in the age of progress, and that progress would just keep moving us all forward on its tide. President Obama illuminated the White House in rainbow light, after all, and Beyoncé was on the cover of *Vogue*'s September issue. *Transparent* was a critically acclaimed show on Amazon, and Hillary Clinton had just officially announced her intention to become the first woman president of the United States. But underneath the smooth momentum, I could feel the rumbling, like plates moving.

It occurred to me that maybe it wasn't just being trans, but the precise timing of my transition that allowed me to see what other people didn't. The rules that newly defined my life were not futuristic: *Do not let yourself be dominated. Do not apologize when you are the one inconvenienced. Do not make your body smaller. Do not smile at strangers. Do not show weakness.* The kumbaya narrative of a world without borders, driven by change, wasn't the whole story. I could see it every day, in the way my body got shaped, read it in the headlines, feel it in the edgy encounters I had with man after man: something terrible was always already happening.

Maybe, instead of looking for the men you want to be, you need to face your worst fears about who you are.

Soon enough, nations would be beset by a wave of authoritarian leaders, including the election in the United States of Donald Trump, a man whose campaign for higher office against the first female major party candidate was, in many ways, an open referendum on bodies and the rules regulating them, especially the recent social and political gains made by those whose existence challenged the long reign of white masculinity: women, trans people of all genders, and people of color. Soon enough, a wave of harassment and assault allegations would topple Hollywood executives, actors, and titans of industry. These men weren't dinosaurs. They were everywhere, all along.

But back in 2015, in the weeks and months after that day on Orchard Street, as friends shrugged off my question, the crisis within and beyond me continued its slow boil. So I began to look for a new way to shape my own becoming. I was itchy, compelled in the same way I'd felt, pre-testosterone, when I saw a vision of a man bearded and shirtless, sitting at some future kitchen table, and I knew in my gut that it was my destiny to become him.

Why do men fight? I began to see the question as

a proxy, a starting point, for what I initially thought of as a very personal experiment: If I shone a light on the shadowy truths about how I'd come by my own notions of what makes a man, could I change the story of what being a man means?

Which is how I found myself, less than two months later, boiling a mouthguard in my kitchen, priming it for my bite.

• • •

The brutal intimacies of boxing—between coaches and fighters, and even between opponents—are part of our cultural narrative, and I imagined they might help me address the question of male violence with some ritual and containment. I was a longtime fan, fascinated by Mike Tyson's steroidal press conferences, and the Rumble in the Jungle and the Brawl in Montreal and the War, but mostly by the literary quality to what struck me as a compelling allusion and troubling metaphor for my own experience of manhood: two men, stripped and slowly ground down to their essences in front of a bloodthirsty crowd in a wounding ballet of fists and a losing battle with time. There was an honesty in that violence, a kind of grace that both referenced and eclipsed my more toxic notions of masculinity. I couldn't think of a more visceral way to face it.

I'd pitched a feature story about the men who elected

to fight in white-collar charity matches, and the guys who trained them, to my bosses at Quartz. Through a buddy who'd done the same fight a couple years before, I signed up to train for a cancer-fighting charity called Haymakers for Hope.

As I was nervously loading up on sweat-wicking gear and boxing shoes, I couldn't have guessed how much my struggle with toxic masculinity would eventually lead me to zoom out, asking questions about my own body in space that required me to chase increasingly urgent economic, environmental, and political implications of the masculinity crisis I'd suspected was connected to me, all along.

But, then again, I had been reading the psychologist Carl Jung, who, after World War II, long consumed by the question of what made people evil, or complicit in evil, settled on a single, elegant explanation. He believed that ostracizing any aspect of the human experience, however ugly, created a "shadow" of our rejected bits that we drag behind us. If we do not see that the shadow belongs to us, we project it onto others, both individually and as a culture. To face and own what most disturbs you about yourself, Jung believed, is among the central moral tasks of being human.

I began this book because, though I could not articulate it then, I understood that I could not know why I wanted to break that man's teeth on Orchard Street without understanding, in turn, why he wanted to break mine.

In pursuit of that night under the bright bulbs of the most famous boxing ring in the world, I spoke to executives and academics, but I also interviewed my siblings, and Jess, and the men who punched me in the face and allowed me to hit them back. I tried to look at masculinity with a beginner's mind, and I asked questions even when I was embarrassed, or when my mouth was full of blood, or when I was afraid of looking stupid, or lost, or weak. Especially then.

Why do men fight? This is the story of how I found the answer.

PART I

Summer

Five Months until Fight Night

Am I a Real Man?

Mendez Boxing gym was wedged between anonymous buildings in the Flatiron, under one of those ubiquitous green Manhattan awnings that signal perpetual construction. Though it was just a few blocks north of the office in Union Square where I worked as an editor, I'd never been within a two-block radius—the miracle of living in New York is the way you fashion and refashion each bit of it, until you've somehow made it your own. I circled the block, fashioning it, three times before finally heading in, looking foolish in my brand-new Adidas boxing shoes, pulled-high athletic socks, and neon yellow shorts. "Yeah?" the counter guy with the scraggly billy-goat beard said, eyeballing me. I told him I was looking for an acquaintance, Chris Lewarne, a rep from the boxing charity that arranged my fight.

He didn't know who Chris was, he mumbled, but waved me down the stairs. I nodded back, descending into the bowels of the gym and thinking about how I'd gotten the idea from movies that men spent a lot of time in amenable, intimate silences, laced through with well-placed words that telegraphed deep truths, like the pivotal scene in every drama about fathers and sons. I suppose I had indeed spent a lot more time not knowing what to say since my transition. Silence was a kind of defense mechanism, especially in the halting stop-and-start dialogues I found myself muscling through with uncomfortable male relatives, or other people's fathers.

I felt the front-desk guy's eyes on my back as I hustled away. This was the sort of place I would need to be watchful, to be careful to whom I spoke and what I said. I had already decided that I would not tell anyone that I was trans. I'd decided it deep in my lizard brain as I'd circled the block before walking in, or maybe after I first reached out to Chris, or actually when I pitched the story to my bosses at Quartz, or, come to think of it, back when I'd first conceived of writing it. It was not lost on me that I was a historical anomaly, and that it was a function of a wave of newfound goodwill toward trans people that I'd been able to spend the years since I first went on testosterone living openly as a trans man with few negative consequences (and that trans people who were not white or male did not benefit as wholly from this new friendliness and awareness of our lives as I did). Still, I suspected from the moments that I moved anonymously through space that the understanding that my male friends especially had about my body impacted the way they treated me, and my goal was to go undercover, to embed, never mind to stay safe among men who liked to beat each other up for fun.

In the coming months, that decision would dog me, not least because it highlighted a thorny truth: that, for all the world, I was just another dude in expensive Nikes learning to hit other guys in the face. The relationship between us mostly white men in high-tech training gear with pristine $180 Reyes gloves and the mostly black and brown coaches and (real) fighters using garbage bags to shed water weight wasn't usually tense, but it was classed. Real boxing gyms, dank spots that were actual training grounds for Golden Gloves champs, were rarely open to gangly newbs like me, but a spate of legendary gyms such as Mendez followed a profitable business model that attracted scrappy Olympic hopefuls, washed-up amateurs looking to become personal trainers or to coach the Next Big Thing, and high-rolling charity fighters alike. I learned quickly that the arrangement had an uneasy economy: amateur boxers tired of the grind could charge white-collar guys (and some women) more than they'd ever make on the fight circuit, and attorneys and hedge-fund managers never forced to expose their bodies to risk of any kind could do so for the thrill and bragging rights.

Pro boxing hadn't found a poster child who captured pop culture since Mike Tyson, but the *idea* of boxing, especially among the hip and well-heeled, had entered a new heyday post–*Fight Club*. The sport that produced Muhammad Ali increasingly lacked in both heroes and the deeper social narrative of his era, leaving a vacuum eventually filled by a boxing-fitness craze perfect for Instagrammable moments. As I walked through the basement door at Mendez in 2015, it was clear that the latest converts were a certain sort of Wall Street guy, in an extension of the "wellness as luxury" trend that had also launched the spinning craze Soul-Cycle. (A hedge-fund manager I met at another boxing gym confirmed this. "I would have done blow with a client in the eighties, or gone to a strip club in the nineties," he said. "But now when I want to impress someone, I take him boxing.")

The stink of sweat made my eyes water as I scanned the room, eventually finding my friend Chris, a beefy, smiley Canadian, watching two other white guys in their midthirties pummel each other inelegantly in the ring near the locker rooms.

"Good work, you guys," Chris said charitably, chewing on a toothpick. He wore the classic Adidas triple-striped pants, a Haymakers T-shirt, and a light beard, but was the kind of handsome that required zero styling to appear stylish.

"Thomas!" he said. "I'm so glad you're here, man."

Chris's fight name was the Cuddly Canadian. I'd seen his photos on social media from his fight two years before and knew he was on the board for Haymakers for Hope, a charity that raised money for cancer research by arranging glitzy bouts between brokers and day traders and venture capitalists with no boxing experience. He was the only reason I had a good shot of getting on the fight card at such short notice—just five months before the event. I was still surprised that my plan had worked, that Quartz had invested in the reporting, that anybody would let a total novice fight in Madison Square Garden with just a few months' training. But I was still adjusting to the way I'd been treated since I'd transitioned: the ease with which my ideas were often executed, the ways my expertise was assumed before I'd proven it, the serious faces people made when I spoke, the heady faith the world seemed to suddenly have in me.

To be clear, the Before me wasn't feminine. I don't know what it's like to be wolf-whistled or be told to smile. I was a short-haired tomboy who grew into a swaggering teen, regularly escorted out of women's rooms by mall security. My younger siblings called me their "big brother," but underneath my practiced cool, I was still raised to fear men: men in dark streets or clustered outside bars; sketchy drivers; solo figures on park benches or in parked cars or on trains with their hands moving frantically in their laps. I didn't question this low-grade, persistent anxiety or imagine a world where it didn't exist. Masculinity was, as far as I was concerned, epitomized by my stepfather, whose years of sexual abuse began when I was four and looking at an anatomy book ("These are boy parts," he'd said, a simple sentence that separated any notion of my body from his for the next twenty-five years), and the parade of strangers whose threat crowded my days long after the abuse stopped.

That's just how guys are, I thought, glad to stand apart from their crassness and bulk, even as my body began to feel estranged from me. So what if I had to cross my eyes to look in a mirror?

"Men," Mom said sourly, as we listened to NPR detail Bill Clinton's infidelity. They were holding us back, the bad dads and the mass murderers and child abusers, the wife beaters and the harassing bosses and the corrupt politicians. Not until I was much older did I realize how complicated her feelings were, that she loved men too, and that her anger was forged in that love: obviously for my brother, and her father, but also for the coworkers that stood up for her, the ex-boyfriends, the civil rights activists she marched alongside in the National Mall, listening to Martin Luther King Jr. announce that he had a dream.

Decades later, when I first had to tell her who I was, when I asked her to call me Thomas, the memory of the way she'd said "men" replayed on a loop as I dialed. I'd picked the name as an offering, after her brother who'd passed. "I love you," she'd said, so simple and true, and I'd been so grateful for her, my mother.

All you need to know about her is that after I transitioned and despite everything, what matters most is that she never said "men" that way to me again.

● ● ●

Chris, a lawyer between full-time jobs, had grown out his hair since I'd last seen him and now worked as Haymakers' de facto general counsel, riding his motorcycle to various Haymakers-approved gyms, keeping an eye on fighters' weights and progress, occasionally hopping in the ring himself for fun.

Bearded and swarthy, standing beside him, I felt like the brainy villain next to the hero in an action movie. "This is going to be awesome!" he reiterated, and I nodded uneasily. Then he introduced me to my potential coach: Errol, an impeccably groomed, bald-headed black dude, who looked at me warily. I wondered, self-consciously, if he presumed me a certain sort of white man, or if his assessment was a colder, more physical one.

"Have you ever played any sports?" he asked, which didn't clarify things either way for me, though he seemed a little encouraged when I told him I'd been a goalie, a position famous for drawing only the truly bananas, a quality I assumed would help me in the ring. This was my inference, of course. Maybe he was just glad to know that a guy that was five feet six inches and 135 pounds wasn't afraid of getting hit in the face.

"Let's get to work," he said. "Can you run a six-minute mile?"

Definitely not, I thought. "Probably," I said.

Wu-Tang blared over a bell that rang out every three minutes and the constant *thwap* of men hitting bags, mitts, each other. I did not run a six-minute mile, but I did run three miles in twenty-five minutes, driven by adrenaline and pure terror through a hazing that lasted two grueling hours. Afterward, from the floor, I watched other men's sweat condense on the ceiling and fought the urge to vomit, feeling proud of myself and strange for feeling proud of myself.

"You've got short arms, but decent strength," Errol said, from somewhere above me. I couldn't see him through the sweat stinging my eyes. "I'll see you tomorrow." Then he was gone.

I hauled myself up, and Chris and I sat on the bench kitty-corner to the ring in what actually was companionable silence for a minute or two, but mostly because I couldn't breathe. We knew each other only vaguely, and mostly from social media. We weren't, however, actual friends. Not that Chris seemed to make any distinction.

"You did great," he said, smiling sunnily. That wasn't exactly true, but I'd take it.

"Listen, don't tell Errol I'm trans, okay?" I asked, once I could catch my breath again.

He looked at me curiously, but told me not to worry about it. I meant to tell him it was to not compromise my reporting, but a part of me knew that wasn't exactly true. As we watched a guy across the way do one hundred sit-ups, pause thirty seconds, then do one hundred more, I realized how scared I was. I wore my insistence that I be taken seriously, an inheritance from Before, differently on this body. With nobody challenging me anymore, that drive now just looked like standard-issue male confidence. I felt an acute awareness, sitting next to Chris, of the inches and muscle the other guys had on me, and within their bodies the potential for my own spectacular failure.

After he was gone, I changed furtively in the locker room, listening to two dudes talk about a cross-country trip they'd taken on their motorcycles and hiding my nakedness by facing the wall of lockers while slipping quickly out of my shorts.

"You got a fight?" the smaller of the two guys asked me.

I flinched at the attention. "Yeah," I mumbled, "just a charity one."

"Don't matter," he said. The other guy nodded his agreement, and I couldn't help the swell in my chest.

I had a fight! I walked all the way home, that night, thirty blocks, like the king of New York.

• • •

"The first jab better be a warning," Errol said the next day. I pretended to be in less pain than I was as we practiced keeping our guards up, looking over our gloves, crab-walking around the ring, then turning into position quickly, so as to expose as little of our bodies as possible. This defensive style was cagey, smart. It was about staying safe by keeping your distance, always being ready, never letting down your guard.

I was familiar with the concept.

"I can see you," Errol said, unnerving me, his gloves covering his face. Then he popped me on the side of the head. "But if you're not watching, you can't see me. If you can't see me, you won't be ready. If you're not ready, you'll get hit."

I pushed through one more round, then another. He had me close out the night on the jump rope, which I immediately tripped over. *Why are you doing this?* I could hear my mom asking.

She always seemed to me larger than even the history I read about in school textbooks. She traveled on a Eurail pass with some girlfriends back when women didn't do such things. She'd worked for Ted Kennedy and met his brother John when she won the Westinghouse Science fair in high school. Even after her marriage fell apart and she couldn't find work; even after she moved to a depressing town near where she grew up in central Pennsylvania; even when she couldn't stop drinking—she always seemed one step away from getting back on track, forever one turn away from her best self, the working-class high school girl tutored by the principal himself, she was that full of potential.

A medical "crisis," her doctors explained to my sister and brother and me in the terrible hospital room a year earlier, is a crossroads where the patient either becomes healthier or dies. Mom, who, when she found out that her husband had been abusing me, put her hand on the center of my chest and told me I had a golden core that no one could touch. I knew I was at a crossroads too, fighting for the future that eluded her, working to become the kind of man we could both be proud of. She was in the ICU in September when the nicest doctor of all took us into a special carpet-lined room with a big wooden table and told us, plainly, that she would not live. When she died a few days after, she passed a mighty hunger on to me. Nine months later, it was within me, a hunger that lived.

"He's taking his time with that jump rope," some joker said, and my cheeks burned. My legs were heavy, but sweat poured off me like a second self, washing away.

• • •

It felt good to see the guys nod hello those first weeks of training, even if I was skinny and kept to myself. Soon everybody knew I had a fight, and that made me one of them. So what if I couldn't even throw a straight right? At least I wasn't there for the cardio.

But I was also wary of this new, oddly warrior-like ego. I fought not to fall under the thrall of these alphas and the pride I sometimes felt when they noticed me. Given the thrill I got when another boxer so much as spoke to me, I found it hard to imagine a teenager on earth who could be immune to the spell of male social-ization.

My brother suddenly made a lot more sense to me. He was five years younger than me, an athletic, solitary kid, often spending whole Saturdays alone in his room after a long day at the YMCA, where he grew pro-gressively more jacked, his muscles covering him like armor. On the ice, the man who raised us long gone, my sister, mother, and I watched him hit other boys in the face with little provocation. Later, his gear in the back of the minivan, we didn't speak of bloody noses or body checks.

I knew that Brett's fighting, both in and out of school, was almost always about me, my body, and the girls I dated in high school. He and my sister, Clare, were protective of me as if they sensed that I was not quite like them, even if we did not know we were half siblings, that their father was my stepfather, until we were adults.

"When I was younger, I was lonely," Brett told me much later. It turned out that the sheen of our childhood, the legacy of his father, loomed as large in his masculinity as it did in mine.

He found solace in working out and played hockey as a form of protection against the boys around him as much as for enjoyment. "Within that hierarchy," he told me, "I would earn their respect by just being authentic and being strong and getting up faster when I got hit. But I still wasn't going to be invited to their parties."

Despite Brett's muscle, he'd long had a distaste for macho guys, and macho-guy stuff, no matter how mocked he was for it.

"At some point, I became pretty callous," he said about his teen years. "At some point I wasn't crying anymore."

Becoming men had brought up the same question for both of us, the central worry of all sons of bad dads: How to be a man without being like our father?

It had never occurred to me, until I became a man, that my brother had felt trapped in his body as I had in mine.

• • •

Here's another story about my brother: When I'd come out to him as trans over drinks back in 2009, before I started testosterone and when I still lived near him in Oakland, he'd hugged me. "You just make more sense as a guy," he'd said.

Later that night, gin-loose, I'd asked him my very first dumb question about being a man: "What do you do when a guy says something sexist, or homophobic?" I figured if anybody knew how to react, it was him, after all those years he spent defending me.

He shrugged. "It depends on how many guys there are, and how big they are."

"Oh," I said, and we never spoke of it again.

But every night, changing in the Mendez locker room, I understood more clearly what he meant. Boys become "real" by proving their masculinity to other men, mostly through taking risks and dominating others who haven't fallen in line. It was not unlike boxing, where "real" fighters were distinguished from weekend warriors in the locker room by our willingness to get hit in the face. The "real" fighters ignored the "fake" ones, not blessing them with their attention, which is why it was almost embarrassing how much I appreciated two guys in particular, real fighters, who affectionately ragged me most nights.

They were a duo of white construction workers, meaty and nearing middle-aged, who took a shine to me for some reason, even though I rarely spoke. Pulling on their dusty work boots as I suited up, they traded gripes about their union, foremen, and job sites, pausing to greet me whenever I showed up with a jolliness I assumed at first was sarcastic. It wasn't.

Still, I couldn't shake the feeling that their interest in me was based in something false, some agreement I'd entered into by not making myself more fully known. I suspected that the men I typically surrounded myself with censored themselves in my presence because I was so publicly trans—a simple Google search will give you a pretty good biographical sketch—and so I waited at the gym, with morbid curiosity, to either be "discovered" or for my passing to lead me someplace shadowy in myself.

One night, early on, that moment came. It was a Wednesday, and I was late, changing quickly to meet

Errol while the two dudes, teasing each other with a sharp edge that felt dangerously close to breaking into a fight, called each other "faggot" repeatedly. I'd not heard men who weren't gay use that word since high school. I sat rigid on the bench, in the middle of lacing my shoes, shocked into the dawning awareness that my brother was right: I would not speak, I could not, even as they repeated the word over and over, because they were bigger than me and if I spoke, I was sure they would see me for what I was, and I was afraid of them.

• • •

The more I worried over how much I had to appear "real"—real as if I'd had a boyhood spent in scuffles, real as if I knew the language of fathers and sons—to survive in a boxing gym, the more I simultaneously wondered over the strange expression.

The phrase *real man* is at least a century old, which is when it first appeared in print in the United States. Back then, lower-status men worked the land, while richer ones kept a wistful eye on the rugged bodies that they considered themselves "better than." But the concept, if not the phrase, exemplified later by the admiring eyes of tuxedoed ringside fight fans who fantasized about hopping in the ring themselves, is the key to a much older story. The tension between the civilized world and a more "virile" masculinity dates at least as far back as Julius Caesar, according to race historian Nell Irvin Painter.

Her book, *The History of White People*, explores how white men invented race and, in doing so, made whiteness synonymous with the masculine ideal. White Western men have been insecure about achieving—or losing—masculinity, twinning that loss and gain with violence, throughout all of history. Strangely, the idea of the real man has also always been nostalgically classist. According to Painter, Julius Caesar fawned over the warrior-like qualities of his "uncivilized" rural neighbors, a common attitude among powerful men in antiquity. He also believed as many men did that "peace brings weakness" and "saps virility."

I thought, with growing concern, of that man on Orchard Street, and the guys in the locker room. I thought of the bouncer, recently, who grabbed me roughly by my collar because he mistook me for someone else, and the rough agitation that rose through me at this insult, the worst kind of pride. *Do not let yourself be dominated. Do not apologize when you are the one inconvenienced. Do not make your body smaller. Do not smile at strangers. Do not show weakness*.

No wonder I felt like a hologram of myself. I'd been learning, through some cultural osmosis, how to be a real man, after all.

41

• • •

Larissa, a freckled attorney who had that can-do sunniness familiar to me from my time playing soccer with women in high school, was Errol's other trainee, and she outperformed me, a lot.

Still, she cheered me on as I struggled to make sense of what was happening when Errol smacked me in the ear, the temple. Errol said I asked too many questions. My therapist said I "needed to get in touch with my anger." He told me that was how I would "learn to trust life again."

I hadn't been the same since Mom died, that was true.

It occurred to me, those first weeks of training, that the man on Orchard Street tried to fight me because I too was looking for a fight. I had ventured, somehow, deep into the "man box," a sweltering and bandaged thing, a mummy's wrap around my body and the bodies of almost every man I know, stitched with the brutal language that ensures conformity, the outline of muscles pushed into being under the weight of "boys will be boys" and "real men" and "man up."

A *man box*, drawn in the crude three-dimensional style of grade-schoolers everywhere, is used by sociologists and activists in a classroom exercise. Boys are asked what words or phrases go inside it, and what should be left out of it. What they choose is a troubling primer in male socialization: Do not cry openly or express emotion. Do not express weakness or fear. Demonstrate power and control. Do not be "like a woman." Do not be "like a gay man."

But sometimes the box is squared as an office or bounded more invisibly, the tight corners scripting the jocular camaraderie at the back of the bar. Sometimes it is an icy enclosure holding a pair of lovers apart in a bedroom or is framed within a television or a phone or a movie screen. Sometimes it's not a box, but a ring, iced or roped. And sometimes it's the slow circles men make around each other in a street fight.

"Men tend to fight when they feel humiliated, when they feel shamed," sociologist Michael Kimmel told me. (Kimmel was writing books with titles like *Guyland: The Perilous World Where Boys Become Men* before the economic "masculinity crisis" and its fallout.) "You don't fight when you feel really powerful," he said. "You fight when you feel like your power is being challenged."

I assumed that fighting for my right as a trans man to be seen as "real" would be a big part of this story: but it quickly became clear that all men proving their "realness" did so through fighting the policing and shaming of other men, sadly often by shaming and policing them back.

What made me feel "real"? When Errol tied my glove on for me or poured water in my mouth, or when I tripped over the jump rope and had to begin again. I felt real when I asked for help, when I failed, when I was myself.

I did not want to become a real man, I realized. I was fighting for something better.

• • •

Chris seemed worried, watching from the ropes in his motorcycle jacket. He huddled Errol and me close to him after we ran our drills, smiling as always and yet somehow also not smiling. They both hovered over me, Chris with his artful scruff and Errol with his precisely shaved head. Chris said he was still looking for an opponent for me, with the fight just four and a half months away.

"You need to get this guy sparring," Chris told Errol. "Now." I tried to hear the protectiveness in Chris's voice, and not the edge of it—the serious ring of fear.

Errol's solution was to throw me in the ring with Larissa, whom I didn't want to hit in the face, even with pulled punches. The unwritten rule of sparring was that guys were only ever matched with women in the ring to practice defense—even in boxing, the code stayed the same: a man was never to hit a woman, period. Anyway, she was better than me, and I felt unsettled by the image of her head reverberating off my glove in front of the men around me, even as she yelled, *"Hit me!"*— as if we were in *Fight Club*, her glee unrestrained as the other fighters walked by, staring so hard at me my throat flushed red.

Mercifully, Chris finally interrupted my sparring with Larissa one night by hopping in himself. He'd kept up his training since his own match two years earlier, but despite the fifty pounds and six inches he had on me, he approached me with restraint. I still only knew two punches well enough to deploy them: the jab and the straight right. Chris smiled at me through his mouthguard, but my heart still thundered in my throat. I was, to my frustration, genuinely terrified by his size, frozen by his flurries of punches.

Larissa watched and yelled cheerfully for me to "go downstairs" and hit Chris with a body shot. "His ribs are open!" she hollered.

It struck me that I was a man more scared of men than she was. Maybe she'd mastered a skill I lacked, or maybe no man had ever used his body as a weapon against her, as my stepfather had against me, until I couldn't tell where my skin ended and his began.

"Now up top!" Larissa said. I hit Chris harder. I was mad at myself for resenting her instructions, for all of the ways I was failing so publicly, for thinking of it as failing, for letting it all get to me, for not knowing how to let it go. I couldn't get my body to move the way I needed it to. In frustration, I hit Chris as hard as I could in the stomach and saw him cringe. It was a dick move.

It was strange and disappointing, I thought, pulling off my gloves, to see the worst parts of culture jutting out of my psyche like a glacier, knowing I'd only begun to uncover the mass that must lie beneath.

Chris, sweaty, knocked gloves with me as we drank some water.

"Look, in boxing, training is the same for all of us," he said. His sheen of honesty made me believe him. "First, you learn not to react in fear. And then you learn how to again."

"Fear is natural, your reaction is natural," Errol agreed.

I could feel my eyes get wet. I nodded.

"And I will drill it out of you," Errol said, patting me on the shoulder, before leaving to join Larissa, who, as usual, had it in her to go yet another round.

Am I Sexist?

I t didn't take long to understand why the Wall Street dude took clients to hit the heavy bag. While I was surely the shittiest fighter at Mendez, showing up at work with a cut on the bridge of my nose had an immediate effect.

"Hey, champ," guys said with teasing tones that baptized me cool. Walking through our open office with my giant duffel bag, yellow gloves dangling jauntily from the handle, it was seductive and strange to feel so powerful for doing so little. Unlike Before.

Before, my beardless, androgynous body was troubling, unprofessional. I was once explicitly asked not to meet with important clients at my nonprofit job, as the very sight of me might "send the wrong message." I never hardballed a salary negotiation either. And I wasn't ever hired, as I was years later, for my "potential."

Before, I related to the struggles of my female friends partly because I saw the laughable fallacy of equity most clearly at work, where I was treated like one of them.

I could pinpoint the exact turn. Six months into my transition, back when I was still working in Boston, testosterone made my voice low. Really low. So low that I was almost impossible to hear in a loud bar or a cacophonous meeting unless I spoke at a ragged near shout. But when I did talk, people didn't just listen; they leaned in. They kept their eyes focused on my mouth, or down at their hands, as if to rid themselves of any distraction beyond my powerful words.

The first time I spoke up in a meeting at the *Boston Phoenix*, in my newly quiet baritone, I noticed that sudden, focused attention and was so uncomfortable I found myself unable to finish the sentence. The crew of rowdy journalists quieted and turned toward me, a body that was newly sprouting hair and muscle that looked, for once, familiarly male to everyone.

I learned then that I had stepped into a new order of things: everyone in the room waited, men and women alike, for me to open my mouth.

Since that vacuum of silence first made itself known to me, I'd thought I was an ally to women at work. But the experience with Larissa at the gym made me wonder if, somehow, I'd become part of the problem instead.

• • •

Larissa's good-natured goading threatened me because, despite a lifetime of knowing exactly how it feels to be treated unfairly by virtue of my body, I'd been upset to be publicly shown up by a woman.

The question wasn't if I was sexist, but how.

I'd promised I'd face truths, even ugly ones. At work, disturbing patterns came into focus. I kept a tally of how often I tried to get my points across in meetings—a practice I'd honed aggressively in my Before body that had a different impact now. Whom did I talk over more often? Women, at a rate of three to one.

Even worse, as I assessed myself honestly, I saw the many subtle ways I took men just a little more seriously. I was quicker to respond to their emails and messages, more concerned with their perceptions, and more swayed by their arguments.

I thought, inevitably, of Mom laughing in frustration at the "silly" things she'd had to do to be "non-threatening" as a manager at General Electric, such as the nights she hosted dinner parties for the wives of her employees in whatever remote boondock she'd been sent to, befriending the women with her famously good cooking after a long day overseeing their husbands.

And I thought, painfully, of Larissa, hitting that speed bag. She was likely practiced at fighting twice as hard as her male colleagues to be taken seriously. She was unaware of my history. To her, I was just a guy with the gall to think I could learn in five months what had taken her a year.

The truth was, I'd not asked her for advice, despite all she knew, just as I had not once considered that my sister, who called to check in on my training every now and then, never reminded me that she'd been taking boxing classes for years, that she'd sparred and won.

Regardless of my Before body, I had still somehow inherited a bias common to a lot of men. To understand how it operates in the workplace means knowing that it often seems innocuous, according to Caroline Simard, a researcher at Stanford. She and her colleague Shelley Correll analyzed two hundred performance reviews within the same large technology company and found that women were more likely than men (57 percent to 43 percent) to receive what the researchers termed "vague praise"—feedback not tied to any actual business outcome ("You had a great year"). Men were more likely to receive praise connected to their actual contribution to the company. Performance reviews may seem like a relatively benign, bureaucratic measure, but Simard told me they are a powerful indicator of a cluster of similar biases that, taken together, hold women back.

Surely, generally, this behavior is not conscious—

which is precisely the problem. "Even when we think we can evaluate rationally," Simard said, "bias leads us to errors in judgment." These "errors in decision making" result in the thousands of subtle behaviors performed unquestioningly by almost everyone of every gender.

The reach of such bias was troubling and pervasive, but as clear to me as the awful new way I found I could silence rooms that day at the *Boston Phoenix*. Since my transition, I felt viscerally that the world was designed just for me. I was reminded of Eddie Murphy's seminal 1984 *Saturday Night Live* skit "White Like Me," where he goes out in New York in whiteface and discovers a secret world of privilege. In one scene, after the only black man on the city bus gets off, all the white people on board pour champagne and dance, as jazz plays merrily. "Slowly I began to realize," Murphy says later in voice-over, after a white clerk won't let him pay for a newspaper, "that when white people are alone, they give things to each other for free."

At the very least, I received a lot on credit. My voice was just the start. I loved my work and—like many people in my age group—finally found a professional groove in my thirties, when I understood more about who I was, but that wasn't all. The friction between my body and the world around me was gone. Being a man was easy in exactly the places not being one had been hard.

Every day, I was rewarded for behavior that I was previously punished for, such as standing up for my ideals, pushing back, being fluent in complex power dynamics, and strategically—and visibly—taking credit. When I proved myself, just once, it tended to stick.

"We assign more credibility and expertise to men," Simard said. And by "we" she means *all of us*. Harvard researchers designed a test to gauge your personal inclination toward bias. If you're anything like me, you'll also fail it.

I didn't know, until I was a man, how to pretend to know more than I did, how to behave as if I were an expert when I was a beginner. But I did not have to know.

My conditioning began the day I silenced a room just by opening my mouth.

• • •

In this liminal moment, a couple of weeks into my training, I saw how much Jess had been right all along. My "romance" with masculinity, if understandable, had blinded me to what I wanted to see most: my shadow. Being a man unwilling to face the worst parts of masculinity guaranteed that I was passively part of the problem. The phrase I'd heard many men say when confronted with negative male behavior flitted defensively through my head: *But I'm not that kind of guy!*

But wasn't I? As various characters Jess and I met at Brooklyn cocktail parties asked, incredulous in those first few weeks of my training, why I felt the need to not only *box*, but *fight in Madison Square Garden*, warning us about head injury, they looked to Jess as if it were her job—as a woman—to stop me. She would gaze calmly back with that unnerving, placid stare that on a man would be read as aggressive, but on her was "mysterious." She would often catch my eye. *See?*

Jess was the exact wrong audience for this approach. She wasn't afraid of risking her body for whatever she believed in. She told me on our first date that she'd just returned from spending a year in Thailand on an illegal visa, working with human rights groups on the border. While I trained for my fight, she'd sometimes be off the grid, working at a grassroots community center run by truly heroic women in Malawi, and I would quell my rising panic as she boarded planes with the image of her serene face, looking back at my battered one.

Anyway, I came to see that the question of why I was doing this wasn't ever genuine. The doctors and journalists and grad students and account managers wanted to know, but only in Jess's presence. Not a single man, if we were alone, asked me to explain myself. Sometimes, even, I would feel a wave of envy pass over a conversation with a guy mining me, in that masculine way, for details about the training: the hours, the intervals, the routine. I had never been the subject of male jealousy before, not over my body and what it could do, and there again I felt a problematic pride swell my chest. *He's thinking that I know how to punch him in the face.*

Another pattern: the junior reporter that held my gaze as he explained an idea for a story while mostly ignoring the woman editor beside me; the all-male panels at conferences; the advice asked of me by my women friends, the heartbreaking familiarity of the questions: *How do I convince my boss to pay me as much as the men I work with? How do I convince myself that I'm worth it?*

Now I saw it all: the women who stayed up editing after their kids had gone to bed; the women who organized the birthday parties and the book clubs; the women who made the coffee; that it was almost always a woman who acknowledged that I'd helped with a story frame or pitched in on a weekend.

Jess was right. I just had to be willing to look.

• • •

When I hear the phrase *women's work*, I think of Mom, growing up in a small town in central Pennsylvania in the 1950s, the daughter of a mechanic and a homemaker. If she pursued higher education at all, she was expected to attend a teachers college. Even after she got into MIT on a full ride, her father wouldn't provide the financial paperwork necessary for her to attend. So she went to Penn State and earned her degree in physics, then her master's degree, all on her own. She eschewed a limiting script about what being a woman meant, like many other women in her generation.

You have a golden core, she said. *And nobody can touch it.*

"Your upbringing made you a person who, regardless of gender, sounds sure of themselves and is willing to take a risk and fail," Jess said, holding my hand on our couch one night. "That's how your other siblings are too, and how your mom wanted you to be. You've had those qualities your whole life, and you're just being who you are, but how people see you now changes things."

She was right. We were all a reflection of our mom's mask of self-assuredness, the "fake it until you make it" face she'd surely put on in room after room of men in ties making jokes at her expense. All of the professors and small-town busybodies determined to undermine her. She rocketed out of the life that was expected of her, and taught me to do the same.

●   ●   ●

Back at the gym, the "romance" that Jess worried I was having with masculinity unraveled with sweet relief, like the wraps I pulled off my pruned hands most nights.

Errol put Larissa and me in the ring again. This time, I no longer felt ashamed, even after somebody hooted. She looked at me, ignoring it. I saw in her the women I worked with, Jess, my mother, my sister. I saw myself Before, the person I wished I'd been, regardless of the body I had. The person I wished I were now.

"Come on," Larissa said, giving me a chance to be him, "gloves up."

As a group of leering guys gathered to watch us, I saw that she wasn't attempting to humiliate me. She was well aware of the unconventional optics of our sparring. She was simply choosing herself over protecting my masculinity.

We touched gloves, and I felt a rush of affection for her as the bell rang. She pulled out her mouthpiece and said, "Hit me."

Somebody clucked disapprovingly.

I put up my guard, shaking my head, and so she came in with a couple solid jabs, then a hard left hook.

"Thomas, get moving," Errol called.

"Come on," Larissa said.

So I hit her back—jab, jab, and a shitty straight right that still nailed her pretty good. I dropped my hands.

"Why are you stopping?" Errol yelled.

I pulled my mouthguard out. "You all right?"

"I'm fine," she garbled through hers, but with a steely edge of warning.

"There's no stopping in boxing," Errol said.

I put my fists up, and Larissa came at me so hard for the next two rounds I ended up hanging off the ropes, gasping for air. I could see men who'd been watching drifting away, shaking their heads. What was worse than hitting a woman? Being beaten by one. But I was relieved to find that I didn't care.

Larissa smiled at me, a real smile. "You're getting there."

"You're kicking my ass," I answered, because it was true, and because she was my partner.

She punched me in the shoulder, and when the bell rang, she clobbered the hell out of me again, respecting me enough, I saw, to no longer hold anything back.

Am I Passing?

B ut something was still strange about the sort of man I was at the gym, and it had to do with passing.

Passing, in America, brings to mind desperate stories of blacks passing as white in order to escape slavery or the oppression of Jim Crow but, as Stanford historian Allyson Hobbs wrote in her book about racial passing, *A Chosen Exile*, its history encompasses and extends beyond skin color: "The poor passed as the rich, women passed as men, Jews passed as Gentiles, gay men and women passed as straight."

In the broadest sense, Hobbs told me, passing exists because we categorize bodies into social binaries like race, class, and gender, and where there are binaries, there is usually reward (economic, social) and a price (family, community, identity) to crossing over to the "other" side. "Part of what makes passing so much about loss is that the stakes become really high," she said, noting that you "have to have the binary" for passing to become a meaningful strategy.

I am a man, and so I was not "passing" as someone I wasn't in order to gain status and privilege at the boxing gym, or when I walked home alone at night, one of many bodies moving through Manhattan without context—but I understood it. I couldn't telegraph the reality I'd lived: the tomboy years or the queer bars that followed. Testosterone made me recognizable, but the price had a flattening effect.

"I had no idea you were trans," said a date, a coworker, a new friend, a woman at a reading. The tone usually betrayed the real meaning: Admiration indicates that I've succeeded in getting away with something. Disbelief meant they felt duped. Sometimes, people don't even have to speak: I feel in their appraisal a search for a different face beneath my beard, a sign of a life Before. The notion that gender is a birthright is hard for many people to shake, and I am uncomfortable proof that it's not. And if it's not, what is it, exactly?

It was hard to pull apart the strands. I looked in foggy mirrors as guys smacked themselves with cheap cologne beside me, feeling expansive and safe, each "he" a benediction. I understood that I was, finally, being seen.

But seen as what? Though it was a relief to no longer experience a rebellion at the sight of my own face, moving through the world in my Before body had grooved my brain, and operating as if that weren't so— as if those grooves had instead been worn by thousands of wet towel snaps and gay jokes—felt as dissonant as looking in the mirror had once been. There was no language to describe my whole self that didn't put me in danger. I passed in that I allowed others to believe I had sprung, fully formed, into the man that stood before them.

Passing is, after all, a social phenomenon. I did not "pass" when I looked at myself, but I passed when others prescribed to me a boyhood I'd never had. I passed as the man others saw, and I did not dissuade them of their vision of me. I was, like everyone, passing as my most coherent translation. It was a blanket of familiarity that I put over myself, and it kept me safe.

I watched other guys pass too. At Mendez, a wrinkly old-timer coached a skinny, knob-kneed sixteen-year-old, and we all heard the sort of standard-issue clichés his coach issued him, a slow drip of "It's not how good you are, it's how bad you want it," and "You can run, but you can't hide," and "You don't play boxing." Other guys whispered that the kid was overtraining, but he was so underfed and nervous that the other men encouraged him in his becoming. He bloomed under that love, and he was always there, grimacing as he ran on the treadmill, sparring guys he had no business sparring, nodding along dopily to his coach's relentless words. He was as scared as I was, as scared as the guys who'd learned to better hide it, and I was uneasy watching him grow his manhood like a second skin, a cover over his whole body that eventually rendered him haughty and strong.

"It's very confusing to be encouraged and groomed within normative masculinity," sociologist R. Tyson Smith, author of a book on professional wrestling, told me. "You hear these things, like, 'Never start a fight, but always finish a fight.' How do you do that?"

How *do* you do that? I returned to the idea that the opposite of passing was failing. Coming by that failing honestly expanded the idea of what being a man meant. I thought about it when I bit into my mouthguard, and when I broke the unspoken code and shut the stall door in the locker room bathroom. I thought about it when I couldn't find it in myself to hit Errol hard, even when he asked for it. What had Errol ever done to me?

Nowhere did I feel the pinch between my passing self and my actual lived body more than in the dank, toilet-paper-strewn space of the changing room. There I was most aware of my scars and private parts, the distinct ways I failed to pass, if anyone really looked. The locker room, a parade of fragile parts so readily on display, shocked me: the fleshy penises, the yellowed ribs, the furry butts.

AMATEUR

Fuck them, I thought, growing bolder, dropping my towel briefly before pulling on my shorts. My acts of rebellion went unnoticed. Ultimately, a tragic sort of grace kept me safe: My body was unimaginable. Homophobia dictated that men never glance at my dick or admit it if they did. I pulled my boxers on, and the men who'd averted their eyes respectfully seemed to see me again. A few even nodded at me as I grabbed my bag to leave, a visible man rendered invisible in my hairy sameness.

• • •

Still, Haymakers and I went back and forth regarding whether to notify USA Boxing, the governing body of amateur boxing, that I was trans. I was a potential liability in Haymakers' relationship with the regulators, who, I got the impression, were already a little gun-shy about sanctioning fights between boxers who were often older, in worse shape, and lacking in the professionalism that serious fighters had years to steep in.

Like most people I know, I generally have an allergy to talking to people I don't know about my genitals. Nevertheless, others' lack of imagination caused me quite a bit of trouble. My dick, the most sensitive of all my parts, physically distinguished me from the other men, and that alone almost kept me off the fight card altogether.

After a particularly long, painful night at the gym, I had a long, painful email exchange with Chris (failing) to clarify the sticking point in the regulations, a rule that trans people undergo "surgical anatomical changes . . . including external genitalia changes and gonadectomy."

Since I did not have gonads, I could not have them removed, I explained. Chris, clearly confused about what exactly I looked like naked, suggested a phone call. With dread, I agreed to it.

How do you prove that you are your gender? I was not the only man to be faced with that question, but my circumstances made it a less theoretical one. I contacted attorneys from prominent LGBT organizations who forwarded me email chains as they consulted one another, debating my options. Finally, they concluded that, if pressed, I should provide a letter from my physician, as well as my court-ordered name and gender change, all industrial-strength proof of my right to exist as the guy I was.

The name and gender on my passport looped back to letters written by the doctor who performed my top surgery, which was possible because of the therapist who wrote that I was, in his professional opinion, a man, and in acute distress because I did not look like one.

As I waited for Chris to call, I saw that my value depended on someone else's being less valuable: another man, a woman, a trans person who did not "pass." For me to *really* be a man, someone, somewhere, had to not be.

When the phone finally rang, I'd decided to not apologize for who I was. If my body broke the rules, then the rules were the problem.

"I don't have a penis, at least not in the way you think," I told Chris, my sense of vulnerability so exquisite, it alchemized into strength.

I imagined him frantically googling around, trying to understand what, exactly, I looked like without boxers. He was quiet.

"You know what?" he said. "I'm sorry you have to deal with this. I'll take care of it."

I don't know if Haymakers ever notified USA Boxing about me, but Chris and I never spoke of it again.

• • •

The locker room was never more full of slippery, stinking men than during the 6:00 p.m. shift change, when it teemed with actual amateurs, training for the Golden Gloves or a circuit fight. As they undid their shoes, we charity fighters laced up. Our gloves gleamed dumbly, our neon sweat-wicking shorts like a team uniform.

I tried to see the golden cores within the men around me, but they were shadowed by the pageantry. The white guys from Queens mostly talked motorcycles and construction; the black guys from Brooklyn and the Bronx traded training tips; and the brown guys from parts unrevealed didn't talk much at all. The bankers and traders and marketing executives, almost all white, were quick and silent. Only the rich guys who'd sparred the real fighters seemed relaxed. I studied them, wondering what it would feel like to catch the train a few stops uptown from Wall Street and do that hand-clasp, half-hug thing with the guy whose family had to move farther and farther away from the gym because the Saudi oil moguls you worked for kept buying investment apartments in Manhattan that sat empty, as if cratered by a gentle bomb, blasting all the not-millionaires farther and farther afield.

As for me, I could never truly be invisible. That became clear one hot night when, standing in my underwear and soaked in sweat, I tried to not pay any mind to the big guy staring at me as I pulled off my shirt. I thought (hoped) he might be interested in my tattoos, so I said nothing.

The guy, a kid really, asked me after what seemed like quite some time about the two smiling scars that ran across my chest. Though under hair, and covered with a tattoo, the scars were rough reminders of the surgery I'd had to fashion a body that made sense.

I'd met this kid before. I knew his life story because he'd launched into it late one night when we were the only guys left in the gym: How he got mixed up in drugs and almost dropped out of high school, then found boxing. He was nineteen now, living with his parents to save money and going to a state school. He'd quit drinking and smoking because he wanted to go pro, lost a hundred pounds, was a new man, shedding skin, like me. He was sweet, and open with me in a way I found familiar.

I don't know. I thought, maybe, we understood each other.

Injuries were a primary discussion topic in the locker room: whose nose was broken, how long you needed to nurse a dislocated shoulder, who'd had too many concussions to still be out there, who had cauliflower ear, who'd fought through a broken finger, wrist, arm. So when he said, in front of everyone, in that dumb way of nineteen-year-olds, "What happened to you, man?," there was an automatic, animal swivel of heads.

I thought about Emile Griffith, the reluctant champion welterweight from the US Virgin Islands, who was bisexual, but—out of respect, or decorum—no sportswriter dared write about his sexuality head-on. Griffith, whose notorious Madison Square Garden win against the Cuban boxer Benny Paret in 1962 left Paret dead and boxing in peril. Paret had called Griffith a *maricón*, a gay slur, at their weigh-in, and Griffith hit him so hard that he put him into a coma. Their fight, which was aired live, sparked a national debate—not about the brutality of homophobia, or masculinity, but boxing.

I thought of Griffith often, how his fight happened just years before the 1969 Stonewall rebellion. Griffith, who told friends that the world wasn't ready for him. Griffith, passing. Sometimes, refusing to shield myself from the men around me, I saw Griffith, who hadn't initially wanted to be a boxer, but a women's hatmaker, looking on. Griffith, who was attacked as he came out of a gay bar in 1992 by a group of men who beat him with bats and chains. The world wasn't ready for him. He was right.

If I was to be a man, I needed to believe in the possibility of a different kind of masculinity, an expansion that included me. But how?

On the other hand, what was I supposed to do? If I told you that my towel fell, and the whole group of them turned on me, even if you thought it was wrong, would you be surprised?

It was not my shame to take on, and yet I mumbled, shamefully, "Car accident."

And everyone turned back to the work of pulling on or off socks, or tying shoes, or packing bags. The guy's friend hit him roughly in the arm and said, in my defense, "Don't you know that's rude?"

So, as the weeks crept on, what initially felt like a choice to remain "undercover" for the story increasingly highlighted the central tension of my life—when would I stop passing as the man others expected and just be the man I was?

• • •

Chris showed up at Mendez with some good news: they'd finally found a match for me. Though there wasn't another fighter as inexperienced or light as me in the Haymakers roster, Eric Cohen's scheduled opponent turned out to be especially good, so they decided to rematch him with another charity fighter who'd also picked up the sport particularly fast. Eric was more my speed, Chris said, brokering a deal. Even though Eric was over 150 pounds, he and I just needed to get within ten pounds of each other, so if we both aimed for 140, we'd surely hit within the ten-pound range.

I grinned through rising panic. Errol looked stricken. The fight was four months away.

"So, let's get this guy sparring," Chris said, in that same warning tone he'd used with Errol the last time. "Like, immediately."

Chris had his hand on my shoulder, and the two of them exchanged a look blunt with worry. In the background, men bled and hit and sweated, expelling themselves from themselves. Every one of them, whether they knew it or not, was looking for something they'd lost.

Oh, but I knew.

After Errol walked away, Chris called me over.

"Listen," he said, leaning toward me. "While I've got you, just a heads-up. I told Eric that you were trans—I hope that's okay. I didn't want it to be a surprise for him, reading your story."

"Oh." My vision sharpened, a shock of anger tightening my jaw.

"No one else knows, and I won't tell anyone."

"Cool," I said, affecting detachment.

"Errol would be totally cool if you did tell him, you know." Chris looked at me meaningfully. "Nobody gives a fuck."

Whether Chris was right or not about Errol, I walked home that night, thinking about the edges of my own man box, tightening.

• • •

It is not easy to face the long shadow of assimilation in the United States, which is as old as the nation itself; in fact, James Baldwin referred to the refusal of "all other ties" and "any other history" as "the making of an American." It is so much a part of our national history to pretend to be what we are not in our striving that many of us no longer see what we have lost.

"Race is an idea, not a fact," Nell Irvin Painter wrote in *The History of White People*. Regardless, race evolved through a collective complicity where virtually every wave of "white" immigrants learned to shed their old cultures. These "expansions of whiteness," Painter argues, included more and more immigrants and ethnicities until only "people of color" were left behind. My own family background, Czech and Polish on my mom's side and (according to genetic testing) Ashkenazi Jew on my father's, surely involved multiple generations of fierce assimilation into "whiteness," a lineage of abandoning customs and traditions in the hopes of greater "tolerance."

Still, "not everybody passes," Painter, a woman just two years older than my mother, told me. "It's like what Simone de Beauvoir says about being a woman: you're not born into the role, you have to learn it."

None are born understanding themselves to be a man or an American or straight or white. We become the bodies we have, the sum of history moving through us, quickfire, like a sickness or a rebellion.

"How many men are there in the United States of America?" she asked, rhetorically. "There is no one answer for all of them. Some of them are recovering misogynists, and some of them are not recovering. We can't sweep them all together in a lump and say, 'Oh, this will never be done,' or 'Oh, we're just getting started,' or 'Oh, this is done,' or 'Oh, we're getting better.'

"Keep at it," she said.

• • •

And so I did. The night Chris told me I'd gotten the fight, I walked home feeling out of sorts. Not until after I'd showered and eaten my training-day second dinner had what I needed to do become clear to me.

I found Jess in bed, reading a book on the tarot and waiting up for me. She wasn't happy, I knew, with the schedule, but she also told me that she was surprised to find that she liked the way boxing steadied me. The near-daily hard workouts, plus the fifteen miles I was required to run every week, had tamed the wildness that dogged me since before that day on Orchard Street, a hollowing that began when Mom died.

You're present, Jess had said.

I hung my drenched hand wraps over the shower door to dry, which she noted with her eyes. I did many things that drove her crazy, but she was graceful enough to tolerate my obsessive interests because she got on her own "kicks": handmade herbal tinctures and IKEA-hacked dressers, probiotic cleanses and solo trips to Bogotá. She could clean a microwave without scrubbing, make candles as nice as those $65 ones in boutiques in Brooklyn, and holistically cure our pets of any illness. If I asked her if something was possible, her answer was always yes.

"I want to quit," I announced.

"Do you?" she asked, with curiosity. We looked at each other. She was in bed because there was nowhere else to sit in our tiny studio. I sat on the ledge of the only accessible window, taking stock of this starter life we'd built together, this sense that we were collaborating on a much bigger beginning. In this moment, I knew, she trusted me to be honest with myself.

"No," I answered her. I thought of Errol's reluctance, whatever the reason, to put me in the ring, as the lack of faith in me that it was. "I need a new coach."

Jess nodded as if she'd been thinking the same thing. "So, get one."

• • •

I called Chris the next morning. I felt a new clarity: the hot need to protect my body, this body, from undue harm. It was the same feeling that had guided my transition, and my flight from my stepfather, and my sense that men could be better than what I'd learned in those hours alone with him, his hot breath against my baby thighs.

I could sense Chris's hesitation. It would have been easier, and probably smarter, for him to cut me loose then. I wasn't going to be raising any real money for the organization. Plus I would be undertrained, no matter how hard I worked. What if something happened to me? It would be a PR disaster.

"I know I can fight," I told him, actually believing it for the first time. Maybe he heard something in my voice, because he said he would set me up with his old coach, a sunny twenty-six-year-old from the Bronx, Danny Mangual, over at Church's gym in downtown Manhattan.

"You'll like Danny," Chris said confidently. "He builds you up."

I looked out the window of my walk-up, and I could see the man I'd once been, getting chased up the block by the guy in the white T-shirt. It seemed impossibly long ago that I'd thought I could learn to fight and that it would, somehow, make men less of a mystery to me. What I'd really wanted was to become less of a mystery to myself.

The thing about boxing, everyone says, is that you can't hide who you are in the ring. But what they don't tell you is that you also can't hide how you feel. I'd lost my way, and it felt profound to admit that this was part of a larger wave of life events I couldn't manage alone. I wasn't sure which changed me more, testosterone or Mom's terrible end. Both manhood and grief seemed to have turned off and on parts of me without my consent.

"Thomas?" Chris said, and I remembered that he

was there. He said he would take me to meet Danny himself. It was unorthodox, switching coaches on such short notice. I knew Chris would have a lot of explaining to do. "See you tomorrow, buddy?"

"Thank you," I said. After we hung up, I wiped away silent tears, put on my sneakers, and ran along the glittering East River, finally hitting a six-minute mile like a man who believes in new beginnings.

PART II

Fall

Two Months until Fight Night

Am I Wired for This?

My new gym was on a side street a couple blocks from the new World Trade Center, in a part of Manhattan that I never visited. To get there from my apartment, I cut through the red and gold of Chinatown, then past the Office of the City Clerk on Worth Street, among bridges and grooms in gowns and jeans, in another New York.

I crunched through the rice littered by the exit and then, farther on, passed the African Burial Ground National Monument, the site of the remains of hundreds of the estimated fifteen thousand Africans who were "buried" in this area in the seventeenth and eighteenth centuries, back when yet another New York had a bustling slave trade. I passed an IRS office and a Chipotle and a Duane Reade built on top of mom-and-pop shops built on top of Native American land. I passed the R and W and 2 and 3 subway arteries, the teens in pristine Nikes and the middle-aged women on smoke breaks from city jobs and the bankers barking into phones in suits worth my rent.

Church Street Boxing may have been across the street from the Four Seasons Hotel, but it shared with Mendez a proudly no-frills front. There wasn't even a desk, just instructions to buzz in. After the typical New York garble, the door unlocked for me, the mundaneness of my fresh start interrupted only briefly by cardio-types flying up and down the stairwell to the basement. The sweaty group in headbands was part of Church's popular after-work fitness business, which I later learned clogged the gym most evenings to the annoyance of training fighters. I hustled past the sweaty flock, and the selfie-worthy sign that said, in greeting, FIGHTING SOLVES EVERYTHING, and pushed open the door.

The guys behind the reception desk tucked next to the basement door were jocular and goofy and welcoming, signing me in and then pointing out Chris, who stood, just as before, next to the ring. The gym was smaller and the bodies more varied than at Mendez, and despite its lack of windows, it had a brightness that put me at ease. All around us, the walls were papered with photos and newspaper clippings and fight posters of former Church's boxers and trainers. Men everywhere had their arms around one another: a guy and his coach in a magazine profile, an amateur who'd gone pro and his squad in a candid shot, an older guy right in front of me talking low to a younger one who looked exhausted but alert, and Chris, who was currently pulling me in for a hug.

"Hey, buddy!" said Chris, in his uniform of Adidas sweatpants and a Haymakers T-shirt, both arms around me, none of that side-hug bullshit. Then we watched two guys who'd just hopped in the ring spar loosely, without the seriousness required at Mendez. The smaller one was like a bulldog, rushing the slightly bigger guy, who moved fluidly beneath his swings.

They both pulled punches and paused from time to time to talk. The bigger one touched the smaller guy's headgear with his gloves at the end of each break, affectionately, though he looked like the younger of the two. At the end of a couple rounds, they took a break for water. "There you go," the bigger one, clearly the coach, said. Then he spotted me. "Yo, is this Tommy?" No one had ever called me that before, but I nodded. Sure, I was Tommy.

"Let's get you in the ring, brother," he said easily, handing me his sweaty headgear and a cup to put on. He was handsome in a baby-faced way, a sprinkle of a beard over what I would learn was a near-permanent grin.

"I've not sparred much," I told him, bracing myself for his reaction.

"Well then, let's go," he said. "No time like the present."

"This is Danny," Chris told me redundantly, somehow already tying the padded headgear around my skull as Danny tightened my gloves and squared the knots, then fished through my bag for my mouthpiece and put it, gently, into my mouth.

"Everybody's scared the first time," Chris said, leaning in close. He'd told me once that his first proper spar, his knees buckled. "You're having a rush of adrenaline. Just push through it."

"We're going to spar every night to get you ring experience." Danny looked me in the eyes to make sure I understood. "It'll get easier, and you will get used to it." He held up his hands as if they were mitts. "Jab."

I did.

"Cross."

I did.

"Great. Feel all right?"

I nodded. I had never been more scared in my life.

"It's just sparring," Danny said, like *No big deal*, holding the ropes open for me. From door to ring it had been less than five minutes, but I already trusted him, and so I climbed through.

• • •

"Thomas has balls," I heard Danny say to Chris at the ropes, after I knocked gloves with the smaller, bull-dog guy Danny had been sparring with a few minutes before, another Haymakers trainee, a quant fund manager with an expensive haircut named Stephen Cash. Any unease I felt about the compliment was eclipsed by my focus on Stephen, who bared his teeth at me from across the ring.

Waiting for the starting bell, he hopped on his feet and tapped out a few combinations on the ropes, breathing through his nose like a bull. The drama was meant to intimidate me, and it worked. I straightened my spine, then promptly short-circuited as the bell rang and he charged me with an impersonal fury.

Who *was* this guy? He was merciless, and a little crazy, pouring on so much pressure that I had trouble moving off the ropes. He muscled in close and hit until he exhausted himself and then, alarmingly, attempted a few light uppercuts, clearly practicing for a fight where the goal would be to wear his opponent down and then knock him out. Because we were sparring and not fight-ing, I could feel him ease off after each flurry, letting me catch my breath, but I was paralyzed with indecision, my mind blank.

"Hit him, Tommy!" Danny said helpfully, so I jabbed away, in a dumb and predictable rhythm, while Stephen easily rolled beneath each attempt. Sometime into the second round, I disassociated, and came to in the defensive posture Errol had taught me: my guard up, my elbows close to my ribs.

I didn't yet realize that fighting was mostly about what you did when you were overpowered. This man, backed into a corner, learning how to fight—this was a glimpse of who I was under the rubble of trauma and expectation and loss. It would take me a long time to understand that this first walloping wasn't the failure it appeared to be—it was, in fact, the whole point.

What I was still convinced of, then, was one of the hardest remnants of masculinity to shake: that I lacked some essential wiring, from boyhood or biology, that I would need to find a way to approximate, and fast.

"Yeah, Tommy, you got balls!" Danny said again, a striking perspective to maintain, not only because Chris and I both knew that I did not, in fact, have balls, but also because I thought I was losing. Stephen had me cornered again and was hitting me repeatedly in the head. "Keep moving, Tommy!" Danny said calmly but firmly. I had frozen, yet again, and this time I'd dropped my guard and was just letting Stephen hit me in the face. Danny's voice woke me up, and I moved out of the way. "Yeah, baby!" Danny said. "There you go."

Danny, sensing that I was getting tired, had us switch to round robins. Me vs. Danny; Danny vs. Stephen; Stephen vs. Ricky, a reedy, would-be Olympian who kept his guard down as if he didn't need it and played with us both carefully, like prey. I was bad, but something about the ease of the group orbiting around Danny made me feel settled: the glimmer of kindness in the way Stephen hit my gloves after that last round, the grin plastered on Chris's face, even the grudging laugh of the serious Ricky, who clearly got a kick out of Stephen, who he'd just given a bloody nose. Stephen, for his part, stopped, grinned, and took a selfie.

I had never met anyone else like him.

Stephen was about my age, and I'd later learn that he was a triathlete and former open-water swimmer, a straight guy who smiled a perfect white-teeth smile and wore pointy boots and tight pants into a gnarly boxing gym. His masculinity was more peacock than brute, which I appreciated, though to see him, it was hard to not think, unfairly, of Patrick Bateman, the main character from *American Psycho*. Which is to say, I expected to not like Stephen, with his wolf grin and fancy shorts, but jumping rope next to the ring as I sparred with other boxers that first night, Stephen surprised me by shouting encouragements. He did not know me, but he already believed in me.

It was remarkable, I thought, watching him between

rounds. When he removed his headgear, it was as if he were stripping off a mask. I saw the person behind the man who'd charged me so viciously only moments before. If I could learn to see Stephen for who he was and not whom he pretended to be, I decided, I wouldn't be afraid of anybody.

We sparred for ninety minutes straight, until the reception guys kicked us out.

"You have to make the other guy respect you," Danny said in the stairwell, everyone else up ahead of us. I asked him if he thought I had a shot at actually fighting in Madison Square Garden in two months. He looked at me bug-eyed, reminding me briefly of Errol. But I was done passing as a type of guy I wasn't, I thought with a kick that must have contorted my face, because Danny stopped short on the stairs and seemed to genuinely consider the question.

"I'm not going to lie," he said. "It's not going to be pretty. You need ring experience. But I'll have you sparring every day this week, and anyway, what matters isn't how you do sparring this guy, what matters is where your head is at after you spar that guy." I didn't know what he meant exactly, but I grasped that the sparring was a different sort of test than I'd first thought.

"You have a strong chin," he told me, my first real boxing compliment, "and good speed. But I'll know we're ready when you show me that you can be aggressive."

Freeze, flight. He was right. I didn't know how to look at a man who had done nothing to me and punch him in the face. How do you do that?

"You've got to believe in your punches," Danny said simply, with his big, sunny grin. "And when you spar next week, you're going to put on a good show."

• • •

As we prepared for the qualifying spar, I studied Stephen and the other fighters in the gym who seemed to have no trouble beating the hell out of any random man in front of them, even as I found it so disturbing: the ruthless whack to the kidneys, the precise hope to cause a man's brain to slam against his skull. Feeling my fist's impact on another person's tender body parts, bruising and bleeding and concussing, was not enlivening, it was distressing.

If aggression was genuinely innate to being a man, what caused it? How would I learn it? And if I did learn it, what sort of man would I become?

The assumption that being a man was entwined with assertiveness, if not an all-out propensity for violence, wasn't just limited to boxing coaches. It was taken for granted in any line of questioning I pursued about men. No matter how nuanced their responses, once I drilled down far enough, I inevitably found the same exasperated refrain as to why men fight: they're just made that way.

The most noticeable mysticism about the innateness of masculinity concerned the sorcery of the substance I injected weekly into my thighs: the synthetic hormone that had, indeed, stripped me of my baby fat, redistributed my muscle mass, turned on my genes for facial hair, and made me look, for all the world, like a man—testosterone.

I couldn't argue with its power. In my first few months on it, my body broadened like a comic-book hero, and I found within myself a sparkling edge, like sunlight on water. It was easy to attribute every change to the oily potion I injected weekly into my thigh: the clarity of color, the shortness of my temper, the increase in my sex drive, the charley horses in my quads, the calming of my nerves, the steadiness of my stride. It was stunning, and disconcerting, to become a caricature of a man so easily.

But it wasn't so simple. When I began my transition, was I more energetic because my decades-long depression was lifting, or because I got my entire week's worth of hormone production in one shot, or because testosterone made me that way? Was I more easily agitated because I was hormonally out of balance, or was it the hormone itself? My body, my doctor back then described vaguely, was attempting to find homeostasis. By the time it did, we wouldn't ever know for sure what was hormonal, what was social, and what was the potent mix of both.

Years later, at Church's, I still didn't.

Outside the gym, I knew that the short jump from testosterone to virility, aggression, and power was widely accepted as fact. In the years leading up to my training, there'd been an uptick in marketing campaigns directed to men with "low testosterone," and a study published in the *Journal of the American Medical Association* found evidence that the number of men prescribed it tripled between 2001 and 2011. A black market had emerged specifically for guys in their fifties and older who cited its "antiaging" properties, despite the dangerous irony that taking testosterone you don't need can leave you deficient in it by switching off your own production. Bodybuilders have been busted for injecting it, women athletes have been accused of having an "unfair advantage" for naturally producing too much of it, and rarely does anyone question testosterone as the immovable biological force in everything from violence to hypersexuality.

I thought about what my doctor had said about homeostasis every night that week before sparring. Along with learning a truly sloppy approximation of a left hook and a few easy combinations, I worked on a much harder skill, the one Danny immediately identified as a core weakness: my difficulty "coming forward."

When Danny told me to be aggressive, he said it as if that impulse should come naturally to me. "Touch gloves like you mean it," he'd say when we'd practice the customary greeting at the start of the fight. "Hit them hard, throw him off."

But it didn't come easily. So as Stephen focused on intimidation, I had to come up with an alternative. What did I want to do after I went back to my corner, while we waited for the bell to ring to start the round? Would I look right at my opponent or be relaxed and nonchalant, leaning against the ropes? Would I practice some combinations to get loose? Whatever I did, Danny said, it needed to not involve what I was currently doing—looking scared as hell.

So, I settled on jumping on my toes, being a ball of energy. If it wasn't intimidating, exactly, it discharged some of my anxiety and made me "look busy," per Danny's constant suggestion.

"That's good," Danny said charitably. "It looks like you're not going to get tired."

Once I opened myself up to learning what I didn't know, I found the men I trained with to be generous teachers. When I fought Stephen, I practiced weathering his storms and hitting back. When I sparred with

Ricky, who was as fast as a panther, boxing with his guard down and in a garbage bag, I practiced launching an offense and then preparing for his rapid countering, not letting him back me into the ropes. With Chris, who muscled me around but played slow and dumb, I practiced seeing what he was actually doing. And when I fought Danny, he focused each sparring round on a lesson I needed to learn, almost all of them psychological: how not to burn out, how to hit back, and, always, how to come forward.

I recognized the process from my time teaching writing. He was scaffolding, cramming a year's worth of training into a week. Charity fights weren't about making beautiful boxers, he told me. They were about getting guys with no experience emotionally and physically prepared to whale on each other for three two-minute rounds. Defense, which was almost all I focused on with Errol, was secondary. This wasn't the time to be shy. Taking the risk of putting your body on the line was the point, even if you got clobbered. Whatever was blocking me from that, in Danny's view, was a problem that needed fixing.

"You're not terrible," Danny said the third night, which was basically a compliment. "Ask me questions," he said, drawing me out. "You can ask me anything."

I was hitting the mitts with him while Stephen warmed up, getting ready to spar somebody new Danny had lined up for me, an amateur with a fight coming up, looking to work on his defense.

"I don't understand how to not feel like I'm losing when Stephen is kicking the shit out of me," I mumbled.

"That's a fight. It's anybody's fight, you never know. He punches you, he has you against the ropes, and then bam!" Danny hit me gently on the side of the head. "You're counterpunching, you're using his own energy against him." Danny showed me how to slip a punch and use the motion to hit back. "These charity fights, nobody gets knocked out, really. You win on points. Bunches of punches. You need to hit him more than he hits you. Don't think about winning or losing, think about punching." Danny looked at me, like, *Get it?* I nodded.

What I didn't say: It wasn't that I was afraid to hit Stephen, or anyone else. My deeper fear—thinking of my stepfather, who wanted to annihilate me in ways worse than death—was that I wouldn't know how to stop.

• • •

Long before I learned to box, as I was preparing to begin my transition, I didn't want to do too much research into what testosterone actually did, afraid of what I might find. The heat in my fists during that near fight on Orchard Street, juxtaposed against my initial failure to be truly aggressive when it counted during sparring, had only confused me further. Did I want to believe that the medical intervention that kept me sane also conscripted my body to a primal, reactive violence? If it didn't, why men were disproportionately prone to violence became an even more disturbing question.

"A lot of people think that males have testosterone, females have estrogen, and therefore males are more aggressive than females," Barry Starr, a geneticist at Stanford, told me. But such a simple, if popular, argument is reductive; ultimately, he said "that's an over-emphasis of biology and an underemphasis of nurture."

In fact, neuroscientist Robert Sapolsky, also of Stanford, told me that the single biggest misconception people have about testosterone is "that it 'causes' aggression."

The classic view, he said, is that high testosterone and social dominance are connected. But, as his studies of primates show, it's not always true that high testosterone and high rank go together. In fact, "you find the highest T in jerky adolescent males who are starting fights that they can't finish."

In humans, if testosterone is raised to an artificial level, as in steroid abuse, aggression levels rise. But for men with testosterone in the normal range, Sapolsky told me, "there is remarkably little evidence" that knowing which man has the highest testosterone levels predicts which is the most aggressive.

"Testosterone doesn't 'cause' neurons that mediate aggression to suddenly start firing from out of nowhere," he said. "It makes them more sensitive to inputs that stimulate them."

So why do so many of us misunderstand the relationship between testosterone and aggression? Sapolsky pointed to an oft-overlooked nuance in the work of American researcher John Wingfield. Wingfield showed that testosterone increases not aggression, exactly, but the likelihood that *men would do whatever they needed to maintain their status* if it was challenged.

Sapolsky said that most hierarchal species respond with aggression to status challenges, "but in humans, you see how powerfully the 'whatever' of 'whatever is needed to maintain status' can dissociate from aggression." He pointed to studies rooted in economic games where winning requires being more cooperative and pro-social. "Testosterone makes people more generous in that realm."

But studies demonstrate that the myths about testosterone impact those games too. Men who were actually given more testosterone became more generous, but men who merely *thought* they were operating with elevated T became less effective and more competitive.

"If our world is riddled with male violence, the core

problem isn't that testosterone can often increase levels of aggression," Sapolsky added. "The problem is the frequency with which we reward aggression."

• • •

Danny was a big fan of shadowboxing, and that I never quite got the hang of it almost feels like too obvious of a metaphor. Stephen, on the other hand, was fantastic. When we sparred, I had the uncanny feeling that if anyone was my shadow in the Jungian, rejected-part-of-the-self sense, it was him. He was unbridled id, both in the ring and outside it.

"I've always been a fairly aggressive person," Stephen told me one night, not exactly boasting. "I got into fights as a kid, I've been in bar fights. I wouldn't call myself violent, but I certainly didn't have an aversion to mixing it up."

I would learn, and not be shocked, that Stephen's reasons for taking up boxing, at least consciously, were less complex than my own. "I found so many parallels in my life to fighting in the ring," Stephen said. "Life in New York City is tough. I mean, everything is a fight, from getting a seat on the subway to a drink at the bar, or finding an apartment. And managing a hedge fund can be a real dogfight too."

Stephen's wild, self-taught style, the subject of much talk among some in the gym, felt too vulnerable to me for such a pat explanation. He recorded and watched his own matches with the zeal of a world-class athlete, not a rich guy fighting for charity.

He was fascinated with Mike Tyson, whose high voice and soft lisp belied a notoriously brutal boxing style and a surprising level of macabre self-awareness. Tyson is still a powerful proxy for a certain kind of American masculinity, a Shakespearean figure whose epic downfall—a rape conviction, a failed "comeback" featuring the notorious ear-biting of Evander Holyfield, and an increasingly pathetic series of fights that ended in cocaine abuse, bankruptcy, and a payday "exhibition tour"—highlighted our collective expectations of the most visceral, primal kind of masculinity, as well as his own. "I am a violent person, almost an animal," he yelled hysterically at a 2000 press conference. "And they only want me to be an animal in the ring."

Stephen, like Tyson, twinned violence with winning, and winning with scrappiness. As I got to know Stephen, his story became more complicated and less clear to me. For instance, I'd assumed he came from money, but he told me later that his mom was from a "shanty village with nothing" in the Philippines, and his father escaped a rural town in western Kentucky that "nobody gets out of."

It was easy to dismiss him for his bombast, but not

his kindness, which was as relentless as everything else about him. Wherever I was that first week, he was right behind me, telling me I had it in me to beat him, even as he kicked my ass. After our third time in the ring together, I felt safe enough to blitz him, and when I nailed him in the eye, he hugged me. If an alien had landed in that boxing gym and had to describe the behavior of male humans, surely it would have concluded that we touched each other as much in love as in violence—that the former, in fact, inspired the latter. If anything appeared "innate," it would surely be the affection between us.

Aggression comes from Latin: *ad* (toward) and *gradi* (walk). Its original meaning wasn't "attack" but, just as Danny kept encouraging me to do, "to go forward." "I'm just never going to stop," Stephen said, explaining his style to me one day. "It's the same way I approached my career, I'm just never going to give up. I got knocked down plenty of times, and I got fucked up plenty of times in the ring. I was a constant moving force, always coming forward."

That, I understood. At home, I often felt inert, and isolated. But at the gym, Danny and Stephen and the rest of the guys called up that force in me, like magicians, and I allowed it—not, I realized, because it was gendered, but because it was necessary. *To go forward*.

In the ring itself, moving toward someone trying to hit me wasn't about testosterone or muscles or boyhoods. Increasingly, I stepped into a coming jab—not ashamed, but protective. This too was all about context, after all: These men weren't hurting me. They were showing me how to live.

What If I Fail?

The qualifying spar took place at the very edge of winter. If I couldn't win, I told myself, as I walked through Chinatown early on Sunday morning, at least I wouldn't die.

I knew I was of particular focus: I started late, trained less, sparred next to not at all, switched coaches the week before, and was matched at the last minute with a guy who had at least ten pounds on me. Danny reminded me, daily, that my only job was to "put on a good show." But we both knew that if I couldn't hold my own, I wouldn't be cleared to fight.

When I arrived, Haymakers had shut Church's down, so the regulars were gone. It was just us charity guys in our fancy gear, half-jacked and mostly male. Guys bounced on the balls of their feet. A lot of fighters talked cheerfully to their opponents, and coaches shot the shit along the walls, hanging back and watching.

Eric arrived and I made a split-second assessment: He was definitely heavier than me, though shorter, which meant I probably had better reach—an advantage. We both sported beards, and he wore a backward baseball cap. In contrast to the jovial mood, he sat by himself in stony silence. I, meanwhile, tried not to look as scared as I felt.

The vibe was strange, as most of the fighters seemed to struggle with the masculine expectation that required they both not take things too seriously (the "civilized" take: "It's a charity match!") and that they prove to the other guy how serious they really were.

Errol was also there, looking more somber than the rest of them, with Larissa. When he texted me to ask what he'd done wrong, I was sorry for the casual way I'd told him I'd found a new coach. It didn't cross my mind that I was, effectively, firing him, and I hadn't even had the decency to tell him why.

I was surprised at my own thoughtlessness, and the foreboding I felt seeing him. I'd assumed, as I'd been trained to, that he'd shake it off. He was a guy, wasn't he?

But I could see, in his striving and perfectionism, the way he also did not quite belong. He'd been hard on me, but not unkind: he'd called me "champ" and checked on me when I was sick. He was even, when I'd dropped him, arranging a sparring session with a coach at a different gym, no easy task. It was easy to tell myself a story about how he'd let me down because he didn't see me, but that wasn't quite true.

Watching him huddled up with Larissa reminded me of the moment after our core drills, a week before our last training session, when Errol stopped me on my way to the locker room.

"If I was a bit of an asshole just now, I'm sorry," he said. "I had a tough day."

I'd been so stunned, I hadn't responded. I could count on one hand how often a man had apologized to me, for anything. In that moment, when he offered a different side of himself, I hadn't met him there. I hadn't asked, though I still wish I had, what he meant.

Now we looked at each other from across the gym like awkward exes. This was his second year coaching, and he'd only get new clients if alumni of the organization had good experiences. I didn't know what his plans for himself were, or if my actions had compromised them.

It occurred to me then that perhaps all of those silent movie moments between fathers and sons were the natural by-product of bodies built on honor and its antecedent, shame. To tell another man how you feel is too risky—if it fails, you're left exposed. It struck me as impossibly sad that, so often, near silence was the only witness men could provide one another without being policed. Why didn't I know this man I'd spent dozens of hours with? Why didn't he know me?

When we caught each other's eyes, I wish I could say that I walked up to him, that I found the right words, that I was the man I wanted to be. But I avoided him.

Finally, he approached me. "Hey, champ." It was a grace, a well-placed phrase—brave. I saw him with sudden clarity: Errol, who somehow taught himself to box much later than the other guys, then fought in the Golden Gloves. We were both outsiders, both fighting to be here, and he'd shown me more about how to navigate this world than I realized. If only we could have talked about it.

• • •

Meanwhile, as we waited for the matches to begin, the charity had us record promotional videos in the back room to play on the JumboTron on fight night. We each hit the heavy bag and shadowboxed in the ring and did sit-ups while two guys with video cameras trailed us, creating a montage that would later be set to silly, dramatic music with the voice-overs announcing who we were and what we were fighting for. Standing in line to record my message, I was self-conscious, struggling to take myself seriously as I imagined the handheld-

camera video of me walking down the darkened hallway from the locker room to the gym floor playing in
the Garden.

Mostly, I didn't know how to explain my presence.
I cared about "knocking out cancer," as I overheard
someone else say in earnest, but I couldn't figure out
a sound bite that would capture what drove me into
this surreal world. Eric went ahead of me, and when
he was prompted by the guys behind the camera in the
back room—"What are you fighting for?"—I heard his
answer: "I'm fighting for my father, who was diagnosed
with throat and mouth cancer about a year ago, and for
all the other improbable victories out there."

I wondered if his dad would be at the fight, and
what it might be like to see a man who taught you to
shave, and who cared for you, die. I thought of my own
stepfather, the only father I'd known, and felt the sting
of orphan's grief that, I realized, also possessed so many
of the men around me: men with dying dads, bad dads,
disappeared dads.

I wasn't sure if beating me was one of the "improbable victories" Eric referred to, but I didn't get a chance
to talk to him—when he shuffled past me, he didn't
look my way. I was suddenly uneasy.

"When men fight, they have to believe that the target of their aggression is a legitimate target," Michael
Kimmel, the masculinity-studies expert, explained. In

Eric's unreadable sullenness, I couldn't get a sense of what knowing that I was trans meant to him.

"Did you ever wonder why so many men who believe that testosterone propels men's violence, why they beat their wives up but not their boss? Your boss makes you feel like shit, your boss is an asshole—why don't you beat him up? Because he has power over you, that's why. He's not a legitimate target."

A "legitimate target," Kimmel said, is someone men feel entitled to dominate—someone seen as weaker, someone who has less power than them. For the worst sort of masculinity to work, "real men" prove their worth by targeting people they can beat. Real men win. And the losers?

I tried to shake off the thought.

"I'm fighting to destroy cancer," I said abstractly, when it was my turn. The guy who followed clapped me kindly on the shoulder. I appreciated the gesture, even as I realized that my discomfort looked, perhaps, like a run-of-the-mill case of the nerves when, in fact, it was a more complex anxiety. I didn't belong here, among these hedge fund managers and Golden Gloves winners. How could anyone think I did?

As Eric pulled on his cup, I scanned the posters of Ali and the newspaper clippings papering the walls, worried that the idea of being publicly beaten by me might antagonize Eric beyond what the people in this room had prepared for. That was the subtext, conscious or not, of why he'd needed to be informed in the first place. I didn't know him at all, but I knew that I was a potential humiliation for any man whose masculinity was measured in shame.

"Tommy," Danny said, appearing beside me, tightening my gloves. "It's just another day of sparring, all right?" He knocked my headgear playfully with his fist.

Keep it in perspective, Mom said, and I nearly fell over, her voice as clear as the wallop of adrenaline, surging through me.

Danny, assessing me, held up his hands again, as on that first night. "Jab."

I did.

"Cross."

I did.

"Great. Feel all right?"

I nodded. It wasn't true, but it had to be. Danny held the ropes apart for me, and even though I wondered if this whole thing was a mistake, I was an object in motion, and so I stayed in motion, a principle of physics I learned as a kid. I was a beginner grabbing the ropes, I was a body pushing through.

● ● ●

We were paired with our future rivals for two rounds, four long minutes. The Haymakers leadership surrounded the ring, taping the match with their phones. Danny, Larissa, Stephen, and Errol looked on as I bounced up and down. Eric stared at me blankly as the bell rang.

It was, predictably, a disaster.

Within ten seconds, Eric hit me so hard I saw shimmers of light. I was nervous, jumping around, wasting energy, while he controlled each round from start to finish, chasing me around the ring. A few times, he held me against the ropes with one glove and hit me, again and again, a straight right to the face.

Between the coaches and fighters and Haymakers staff, probably fifty people were in the gym, but I couldn't hear a thing: No hollering, no cheering, nobody jumping rope. It was near-silent as Eric charged me. I was, I realized, not just losing.

I was being beaten.

Errol's face, worried, smeared across my peripheral vision. But a moment later, near the end of the first round, Danny caught my eye and smiled.

It's just sparring, he mouthed, and I nodded back.

I can do this, I thought, just as Eric lunged toward me and I tripped over my feet and fell dramatically to the floor.

It was humiliating and, by the rules of a charity fight, it was a knockout. I bolted back up, pushing myself off the mat with my gloves and shook it off like a dog. It hit me physically, a bodily response to threat: I actually wanted to fight.

I could hear Danny yell from my corner of the ring, "You all right?"

I waved him off. All I had was my strong jab, my shaky right, a week of sparring, and my confidence. The worst had officially happened. I swung wildly at Eric until the bell rang.

Danny told me to keep it up, pouring water into my mouth. I was surprised to see that the other fighters had gravitated to the ring, and I saw a few friendly faces, guys who worked or trained at Church's, who'd come in early on a Sunday not to work, but to watch. When the bell rang again, some of the men I knew shouted directions at me: "Up top" or "His ribs are wide-open." I felt lighter, not like a failure at all. I hit and hit and mostly missed. But the guys watching weren't embarrassed for me. They were cheering me on.

I looked Eric in the eyes even as he hit me. However bad I was, my hands flew, like a chaotic flurry of birds, in Eric's general direction. I did not hate him, and I did not win. But I didn't give up either.

Afterward, I half crawled out of the ring, and the old-timers and the coaches gave me high fives. I was awash with adrenaline making me sick, just as Chris had told me it would. "That wasn't, like, my proudest moment," I said, even as I realized that it was.

Danny, meanwhile, looked at Eric with utter derision, and I felt such affection for him I wanted to cry.

"You did great," he said. "This dude, Eric, has got no skill. He's telegraphing every move."

We were silent for a moment, contemplative. I was slick with sweat, still ragged with fear, and happier than I'd been since the terrible last weeks of my mom's life. I felt her beside me, asking lightly with those raised eyebrows of hers what the hell I was doing, but she was always already on board. She had taught me how to dream myself into being.

"I'm not worried," Danny decided. "You fell down, but you got up." He looked at me approvingly. "That's the story of what just happened. That, we can work with."

• • •

Fighting every day softened violence in a way that demystified it. It came as a relief to me to learn in real time that summoning "aggression" was less about the other guy than accessing the fight in myself, the very human will to live.

Still, my male body didn't always communicate that dawning awareness in the way I intended.

"Check out my jab!" I said proudly to Jess one night, practicing in the bathroom mirror.

"A man on the street followed me for blocks today, saying, 'I want to fuck you and to kill you,'" she said,

AMATEUR

pointed but not unkind. I lowered my fists. She didn't
like when I shadowboxed at home, even in play. She did
not want to be reminded that I could be a man worthy
of fear.

I understood. One night, walking down Second
Avenue, I tensed up at the heavy footfalls of a man coming up behind me. I was alone on my side of the street,
and despite my boxing training, I did not formulate
any sort of plan for fending him off. Instead, my body
locked in place, collapsing back into a night in 2009 in
Oakland, when a man tackled me to the ground on 41st
Street and held me at gunpoint for ten long minutes.
Later that summer, he shot two other men in two separate robberies, killing one. He let me live, I'd come
to believe, because when I spoke, my then-higher voice
betrayed that I was not yet male. Now, as this panting
man drew near, I stood still, waiting for whatever terror was to come. I closed my eyes, and when I opened
them again, he was in front of me, striding away in his
Nikes and sweatshirt, looking like the guys I trained
with, looking like me on one of my biweekly runs.

Jess's comment reminded me of that moment, and
another. Running along the East River in my own
hoodie-and-track-pants uniform at dawn, I'd been too
absorbed in making my time to notice that the woman
ahead of me was the only other person around. I closed
the space between us, thinking that I had another shot

at a six-minute mile, thinking of the shower I'd take when I got home, thinking about the sunlight on the water, the boats under the bridges, everything but how it must have felt for her to hear me coming as we approached the most desolate part of the running trail, until I was just a few feet away and she looked back, a quick assessment, and I saw a panic in her face so familiar it rocked me, and I slowed my pace to a near stop, until she was far away again. I stood at the spot where I'd once thrown a letter to my mom into the East River, watching the water and wondering if it was possible to break your own heart.

The next time I found myself behind a woman running alone, I thought, I would do what I wished men had done for me: I would announce myself. "Passing on your right!" I'd call. I would be careful to give her a wide berth. I would be aware that my body was, for much of the world, a weapon until proven otherwise.

People sometimes think that being trans means I live "between" worlds, but that's not exactly true. If anything, it has just created within me a potential for empathy that I must work every day, like a muscle, to grow.

• • •

I bought a bigger gym bag to lug around all the things I had to carry: sixteen-ounce boxing gloves for sparring, twelve-ounce gloves for hitting the pads, wraps, socks, shorts, shirt, running shoes, boxing shoes, sweatpants, water bottle, sweatshirt, mouthguard, headgear, jump rope. It was like holding a whole other life alongside my workbag, with its laptop, packed lunches, and notebooks.

At work, I kept up my tally of whom I talked over, and why. I asked my coworkers for feedback. At the gym, I spent hours each day learning how to slip and use the latent energy to counterpunch. At work I focused on collaboration. When I ran meetings, I opened with a question so that everyone else in the room felt safe to speak. At the gym, I learned that each of my inhibitions could be surmounted, whether it was lifting ten more pounds or summoning the energy for a final flurry at the end of a long round.

I was quieting, rooted to the ground, and less impulsive about making a show of it. I ran five miles in forty-five minutes and saw that I had underestimated myself. I was relentless on the speed bag. I saw my flaws as mutable facts, like shadows brought to light.

When I wasn't at the gym, I watched YouTube ballets of men hitting men. I saw the transcendent beauty in all of it: Muhammad Ali moving his massive body with feverish grace; Manny Pacquiao's infectious, crazed energy; Floyd Mayweather's caution and tactical intelligence; Mike Tyson's bravado, his madness, his insistence on himself. Each man had a weakness that he'd turned into an advantage: Ali's inability to demonstrate the "right" form also meant he reinvented the language; Pacquiao's small size gave him speed and heart; and Tyson—well, the man said it best: "I can't be beaten unless I do it to myself." His brutality could compensate for his short reach, but he was his own worst enemy and his biggest fan.

And mine?

Once, when Danny was late to meet me, a graybeard, chicken-muscle guy I'd never seen around tottered over to where I was working the bag, pulled off his own glove, and lifted my elbow an inch. "Your hook is crooked," he said. There were a lot of old guys like him at the gym, guys in fedoras and tracksuits, guys who'd stayed in Las Vegas suites with champions or wanted you to think they had.

"I've been watching you," he said. "You've got a lot of heart." This was boxing's biggest cliché and its sweetest compliment. I didn't know what to say. He patted me on the shoulder and hobbled back to his own bag, and for the next few minutes I could hear his sharp exhale as he hit and hit and hit, believing in his punches, telling a new story in the face of his own blatant decay. He had heart too.

My weakness, my advantage, was that I was a beginner, and so I was better positioned to see everyone's vulnerabilities, including my own. I was not ashamed of what made me myself, but I was learning how to protect it. It reminded me of the coyote I spotted once, in San Francisco, walking across a parking lot in broad daylight as if it were a dog. It wasn't a dog, was the thing—it knew it was a coyote. I was the one who was mistaken.

In Native American folklore, a coyote can be both a trickster and a hero. Sort of like a fool, my favorite card in the tarot. I had him tattooed on my chest, merrily falling off a cliff.

"To call a man a fool is not necessarily an insult," said the philosopher Sam Keen, "for the authentic life has frequently been pictured under the metaphor of the fool. In figures such as Socrates, Christ, and the Idiot of Dostoyevsky we see that foolishness and wisdom are not always what they seem to be."

I was a fool, that was my advantage. The fool, the Roman proverb goes, is always beginning again.

Why Won't Anyone Touch Me?

I came home late with bruised eyes and ribs and crawled into Epsom-salt baths. I came home late, mealymouthed, and hung my damp hand wraps over the shower and my sweat-soaked shirts and shorts and socks and even underwear all over the apartment. I came home late and made protein shakes and egg sandwiches and rejoiced in the sweetness of the present moment: the vibrant green of the plants, the feel of the mattress on my back, the sandalwood incense that clung to the sheets.

I made boxing my church, and it calmed me.

Jess said boxing made me less volatile, which surprised me because I hadn't realized she knew I had been so angry in the first place, but I thought with regret back to that day on Orchard Street, and the fights she and I'd had since my mom died—the sort of shadowy events where my maleness translated in a way I didn't understand.

The rules had changed, and so had I. Before, I was a softie, quick to apologize, generally more concerned with keeping the peace than proving a point. Now, I had to work harder to not take things personally, mostly because the translation of hurt or fear or anger through my new body created an impression that often baffled me.

Nowhere were the limits of masculinity more apparent to me than in my most intimate relationships. My abiding fear remained for years after I began injecting testosterone that I would be made strange, and that in my strangeness, I would not be loved.

Though I had been supported by friends and family, something had indeed dimmed. Pretty much everyone treated my body as if it were radioactive. It was easy to blame it on repressed or explicit homophobia in men, or straight women friends' latent concerns about sending the wrong signals in our suddenly cross-gender friendships, but that didn't explain the family members who did not hug me after my mom died, or why, in boxing, guys I barely knew swatted my ass, or draped an arm around my shoulders for minutes at a time. The code of how and why I was and wasn't touched was a mystery to me.

My interest in being held hadn't waned. I couldn't

make sense of what lack of touch had to do with gender. It seemed, to me, a core hunger of being human.

• • •

Of course, that hunger wasn't about physical touch
exactly—nor was it unique to me. But it was still
stunning to discover that boys are not always starved
for it.

In *Deep Secrets: Boys' Friendships and the Crisis of
Connection*, a book by researcher Niobe Way based on
her decades of work with adolescent boys, a fifteen-
year-old boy describes his best friend with the flow-
ery language often associated with teenage girls: "You
have this thing that is deep, so deep, it's within you, you
can't explain it. I guess in life, sometimes two people
can really, really understand each other and really have
a trust, respect, and love for each other. It just happens,
it's human nature."

My surprise at this confused me. Hadn't I had
similar relationships at that age? Why had I not even
known about the intimacy boys shared? Where were
the coming-of-age movies and novels that mined the
real depth of their friendships? And in an era in which
the former surgeon general of the United States calls
loneliness an "epidemic" because of its links to ill health
and even increased risk of premature death, why do so
many men who were once boys, boys who may have

seen their love of their close friends as "human nature," struggle to maintain any friends at all as adults?

According to Way, a psychology professor at New York University, everything changes between sixteen and nineteen (this age range also coincides with a rise in male suicide rates). That's when boys learn that to be too close to guy friends is, she said, abruptly labeled "girlie" and "gay."

Within this limiting context boys learn that violence is the only way available to them to bond. "In a messed-up society that doesn't offer them opportunities for healthy connections, they go into unhealthy connections," she told me.

It wasn't a coincidence that the oft-incompatible extremes of the boxing gym—kindness and violence—gave fighting, oddly, a sheen of sanctuary. Because no one was worried, I guess, about being perceived as girlie or gay, I rarely found my masculinity being policed by the other fighters. The trade-off made me sad.

"If you raise people to go against their nature, which is to be loving, connected human beings," Way said, "if you raise them to believe that somehow there is something wrong with that part of their humanity, why are we so surprised when many of these humans grow up and act crazy?"

Why indeed? Way's words provide an unsettling context to a disturbing piece of boxing history: a 2002 press conference where a wild Mike Tyson screams, "I'll fuck you till you love me, faggot," at a reporter who suggested that Tyson needed a "straitjacket."

If you watch the video on YouTube and freeze the frame, you will see the startled reactions of the men around him, the promoters and hangers-on, shocked that Tyson—the kid with a lisp and glasses from Brownsville who learned to fight the day an older bully broke the neck of one of the pigeons Tyson had so tenderly raised, the teenager without parents, plucked from juvie by a washed-up coach, Cus D'Amato, who moved him into his mansion upstate and transformed him into the most ferocious fighter alive ("I was like his dog," Tyson said), the fighter whose every punch was "thrown with bad intentions," who said D'Amato trained him to "be totally ferocious, in the ring and out"—the men around Tyson appeared positively shocked at what he had become, as if he were an anomaly and not, like Frankenstein's monster, a man built of a long line of masculine expectations, as if he were not behaving exactly as he'd been designed to.

"I'm not an animal anymore," he said in 2005, after cutting short his last fight. "I don't love this no more."

In a 2008 documentary he said, "I just want to be a decent human being. I know I can be."

But in 2013, Tyson told reporters that he was on the "verge of dying" from alcoholism, and that he'd been lying about being sober. "I hate myself," he said to a silent room, stripped of bravado. "I'm a bad guy sometimes, and I did a lot of bad things. I want to be forgiven."

He told the *Guardian* in 2014, "I surrendered." He was five months sober, and he spoke plainly about his grief over the 2009 death of his four-year-old daughter, Exodus. He cried.

"Maybe I'm making progress," he told the reporter. But he was forty-seven years old by then. Mike Tyson, whose self-definition and conditioning has revolved entirely, and for our entertainment, around the opposite of "surrender."

Has he changed? In 2015, he was one of a tiny minority of black celebrities endorsing Donald Trump for president. He told the *Daily Beast* that he was drawn to Trump's drive to win and saw—correctly—that they shared something fundamental in their approach to the world.

"We're the same guy," he said, defining toxic masculinity better than any sociologist I spoke to. "A thrust for power, a drive for power. Whatever field we're in, we need power in that field. That's just who we are."

"I want to be forgiven" is such a different sentiment from the resignation of "That's just who we are." In Tyson's comic and brutal self-awareness, he is an inconvenient and complicated reminder of the depths of the worst parts of masculinity.

His is not a comeback story. It's a cautionary tale.

• • •

Against the ropes has become a metaphor for near defeat in everything from love to business, but in boxing, like life, fighters with good defense can absorb blow after blow, gathering strength in their bodies even as they are laid bare, energy building until they roll out and attack with a deadly combination. *Against the ropes* is the crossroads of crisis, and the best fights are won by defying the odds.

Against the ropes, like when Mom died. Jess and I had just started dating, and she watched me navigate extended family, power of attorney, medical directives, the ammonia in Mom's brain. Jess took my phone calls from the hospital cafeteria, laughed at my stories about sneaking my mom illicit grilled cheeses. They met once, in that terrible nursing home in Pennsylvania, and Jess listened to Mom tell beautiful stories about my brother's hockey career and his art, because she thought I was Brett. I didn't correct her, saving the stories for him, all of the things she'd never told him, locked up inside her. As we left that day, Mom emerged from the fuzziness of her brain to tell Jess she loved her. Jess without pause said, "I love you too."

Jess told me that she knew she'd marry me because of the man I was then. I had never wanted so much to give up, not after a childhood of sexual abuse, not after being mugged at gunpoint, not during my transition, when almost everyone I knew fell away like shed skin. I would stand on my roof, smoking illicit cigarettes and talking to myself or my mom, and think maybe I should jump right off it. Against the ropes: I called my best friend from childhood, my new friends in New York, my therapist. I asked and I asked and I asked for help in my male body, and my anger relaxed against the bodies that held me up.

"Come forward," Danny said over and over, but what I heard was that I needed to fight.

He pressured me back onto the ropes, again and again, until I saw the opening, and I surprised myself by doing what he'd taught me: rolling, coming around the side, hitting him straight and hard in the head. Coming alive.

"There we go!" he yelled every time. "There we fucking go!"

In sparring I became "Tommy"; I consented to violence that was designed to keep me safe; I asked for help in fighting for my body; and other men readily agreed.

Vulnerability was a choice, a risk, an intimacy, both in the ring and out. Like confiding in Danny that I was nervous I'd freeze up, or when Jess held my head in her hands, studying the purple hue of my first real shiner, and asked, "What happened? Are you okay?" I fought the urge to peacock or shrug it off, but I didn't.

Would I freeze? Would I fail, in front of hundreds of people? Danny had put his arm around me earlier and said, "You won't."

I put my arm around Jess in an echo, not pretending to be brave. "I'm scared," I answered her honestly. "And also I'm okay." I was afraid that this admission would make her less attracted to me.

But she loved me, I had to believe, all the more for it.

• • •

Desire is a paradox for everyone, but for most of my life, my body was desirable only when I pretended to be something I wasn't.

"You're like a guy, but better," said the girl in tenth grade—whose boyfriend was the captain of the soccer team—right before we made out. The next year, I dated our homecoming queen on the sly. That narrative—a guy, but better—got me through college, where I grew into my own brand of swagger, binding my chest and spending an entire summer as a barback at Meow Mix, New York's now-defunct, legendary lesbian bar. My type was the woman who not only dated men, but was unhappy with them.

That was a lot of women.

Back then, my masculinity felt cleaner and clearer to me, a solution, not a problem. Being an interloper let me remain recognizable ("like a guy"), while avoiding all the baggage that gender entailed ("but better").

Growing up, I had little empathy for men. Their problems were trivial when compared to those of the women in my life who, like me, had been sexually abused by a parent, or raped, or coerced into sex. Every woman I knew was sexually harassed with obscene regularity. *No wonder they wanted to date me,* I thought. It wasn't hard to be decent and loving, and certainly it was possible to go an entire lifetime not raping or harassing anyone. The "nice guys" I was friends with struck me as whiny and oversensitive. I was "nice," I thought, and I didn't have any trouble getting a date.

When I began my transition, I thought I could still be "better," even if I traded being "like a guy" for becoming one. What I wasn't prepared for, when I began injecting testosterone, was the way the filter of my body changed everything.

"You're a feminist?" dates asked, eyebrows raised. I knew exactly how it sounded.

So began the worst dating year of my life. In attempts to telegraph that I was not a threat, I systematically torpedoed first dates and bungled flirtation. Before, I amplified my masculinity into a wry performance. Now, I made myself smaller, afraid to spook my

Tinder matches, always doing the wrong thing, unable to marionette myself into the right moves, baffled by etiquette I'd never learned, everything a minefield. "Who pays on the first date? No one really knows anymore," a *Wall Street Journal* headline read, capturing my panic. I overthought everything. The gender pay gap made splitting the bill feel unfair, but I did not want, either, to further the antifeminist presumption that I would pay. "The asker pays," a gay friend said simply, trying to help. But that seemed like a relic from a different life.

Then there was the weirdness of dating apps and the strange shame of my dick and how I'd explain it. I tried telling women on the first date. Before the first date. On the third date. "Everybody gets rejected, that's dating!" people said unhelpfully. I dated women who'd been with trans men, but found those encounters just as baffling. Before, I was used to my body breaking the rules of a language I didn't need to speak ("but better"). My newness made dating more like a game of telephone. I tried on different selves, cribbed from movies and TV shows, becoming further from the truth with each effort.

A few months into my new dating life, a well-meaning friend I'd known for a long time advised me that I was being "too vulnerable" with the women I went out with. We were in a gay bar, and my awkwardness in this new body had clearly erased the confident first kisses and the flirty straight girls of my old life.

"It's not sexy," she said simply. My Before self in the initial stages of dating—forward, confident, romantic—felt predatory now. That vulnerability my friend clocked on me was just my desire for connection, stripped of pretense.

So I quit the dating apps and stopped trying to impress straight women who I worried would be ultimately scared off by my junk, anyway. If I didn't find someone who wanted to touch me and really touch *me*, I figured, I wouldn't be touched at all.

• • •

Recently, I was on a panel about masculinity and feminism. Toward the end of a long conversation about bystander interventions, a woman raised her hand to comment, "This whole time we've been talking, I've been thinking about the men I'm drawn to: motorcycle-riding, big-muscled jerks who love to argue with me about everything I believe in." After an awkward silence, she pressed on, "I don't understand how anything will ever change if I keep dating the exact kind of man I don't want to see in the world."

A few people nodded. I told her I understood exactly.

Sarah DiMuccio, an American researcher and PhD student at New York University, published a paper in *Psychology of Men & Masculinity* that offered a simple, cultural definition of that type of manhood that stuck with me. Comparing the Danish idea of masculinity with the American one, she found that the major difference between them was that in Denmark, men said to "be a man" meant not being a boy.

American men said that to "be a man" was to not be a woman.

That is, Niobe Way says, where all the trouble starts. If being "feminine" is the opposite of being a man, then many qualities that Americans associate with women (such as empathy, which shows up in boys as well as girls) are not just frowned upon, but destroyed in boyhood. "You're only a man by not being a woman," Way told me. "That's basing someone's humanness on someone else's dehumanization." I thought of real men, and passing. I knew this America intimately.

Even people who study masculinity aren't immune to the same toxic narratives they work to take apart. DiMuccio, who is from the United States, has a Danish fiancé, and said she struggled for some time with his disregard for American machismo. Yet, like many of us, that's not how she thought she'd react: "If someone asked me, 'Would a sensitive guy turn you off?,' I would never have said yes. It actually took me a long time to turn off the socialization that I didn't even realize was there."

I thought of the woman who'd told me I was too

vulnerable, the failure it implied, the long dry spell that followed. It was a terrible calculus, but a life spent alone seemed better to me than one lived dishonestly. I didn't date again for a very long time.

• • •

The night Jess and I met, deep into my self-sanctioned romantic break, wasn't unlike my other disastrous false starts. A friend introduced us, and we talked gamely for two hours on the dance floor at a warehouse party in Bushwick. I brought us round after round of Jack and Coke in Solo cups, covering up my nervousness by mostly staying quiet as she told funny stories about growing up in Connecticut. She was charming, with a familiarity in her tone as if she'd known me Before, and we were just meeting again. I couldn't figure out what to do with my hands as the night wound down, and I felt the weight of her interest.

"When we were talking on the dance floor, you were kind of icing me out a little bit," she said years later, a misconception that, luckily for me, added "a little bit of intrigue."

But I remembered her ease with me that night, and I eventually screwed up the courage to ask her on a real date. In the intervening years, we too have faced and dismantled gendered expectations, such as when she pointed out that I often tried to fix her concerns about work by giving her unwanted advice instead of actually listening. Dating a woman as a man layered history onto us in a way I'd never experienced, and it took some getting used to.

"When I make a point of being a woman, it's almost always political," Jess explained to me once. "For me, gender isn't the one thing I need people to know about me, because it more or less matches up with how I feel. But when I feel more rigid and gendered in my expectations, it's not ever about gender. It's about feeling out of control. We are all raised to believe that gender is the one fixed thing in life, and it's not."

When we'd first met, Jess told me that she was attracted to people, not bodies. But when I asked her about what drew her to me, and if it had anything to do with my masculinity, I heard myself reflected in her answer.

"When you're being really sensitive and tender, I see that as very masculine," she told me, calling up that conversation I'd had with that friend a long time ago. "When you're being very comforting, or softening the situation, I see that as powerful."

Even now, it is almost inconceivable to believe, but Jess didn't think I was *like a guy, but better*. She thought I was the guy I wanted to be. Full stop.

● ● ●

My personal "masculinity crisis" only began to turn as I practiced doing what men weren't supposed to: asking questions, risking exposure, seeking help, aligning with women, committing to an uncompromised version of myself.

Which, paradoxically, made me more comfortable with being a man. *Tough and tender,* I'd think all the time. I knew the mantra helped explain me to myself. But it wasn't until Chris came by my office in Union Square that I saw how it allowed me to see other men with more nuance too.

He arrived on his motorcycle, and we talked about off-roading, and how he was an adrenaline junkie, and how he got into fighting. As with Stephen, I'd assumed he'd grown up rich because of his sparkly teeth and ease with the finance bros, but he said he was raised in subsidized housing outside Toronto and got jumped a lot growing up. He worked as a bouncer back then and sometimes even went looking for fights. "I've allowed stuff to happen that didn't need to happen because I wanted to beat myself up," he said.

Boxing changed his relationship to fighting, he said. "The chaos is contained and you're forced to confront what is in front of you, because the ring is only so big." Unlike the muddied momentum of a fight in the street, everything slows down. "You have the time to say, 'Who am I?' To say, 'I see my adrenaline, and what is that a response to, and why is it responsive in this way?'"

Increasingly, I felt the same way: as if that boiling inside me could be cooled without losing its power, and in it I could see myself. I knew it had to do with the way sparring had transformed threat into play—an intimacy, like puppies wrestling.

But it was still dangerous, and sometimes I forgot just how much risk I assumed each time I stepped into the ring. One night, a month before the fight, Stephen rushed me and I could see little opportunities for shots—a straight right here, a jab to the kidneys there. I was still terrible, but I was learning to time a slip, to roll out from under punches. It felt like progress.

I heard his awful yelp before I realized that he was on the ground. Danny jumped into the ring and knelt down beside him. He was holding his knee to his chest, lying flat on his back, making all sorts of sounds I'd rarely heard a man make. It wasn't crying, but it was the cousin of crying. It was the sound of a man who needed to cry and couldn't.

Danny got him up, and Stephen leaned on Danny as they came out of the ring while I stared. "Are you okay?" I asked, and could see Stephen flinch at the question.

"I was in rehab for this ankle, I broke it a few

months ago." Stephen winced. I had never seen him express an emotion that wasn't some variation of jocular pride. I could see, as I offered him a hand, that this was what all of his hollering and posturing was designed to hide.

I ordered us a car to get him home—he lived only a few blocks from me. On the ride back, to distract him, I asked a million questions about his job, something to do with creating algorithms for money management, which I didn't understand at all.

When we reached his apartment, I carried his bag and he put his arm around my shoulders. His place was two stories, just a stone's throw from my own tiny studio, a tenement on the border of Chinatown. He had a deck, leather furniture, a giant dog, and a gangly roommate named Ed, who was also learning to box. I deposited Stephen on his couch and asked if he needed anything, maybe ice from the freezer, but he ignored me.

He was going to fight, he told me or himself. He might just need a few days off. I tried not to be grateful for the reprieve from sparring with him. Looking around his huge place, I wondered if his roommate would take care of him.

"Thanks, Thomas." Stephen waved his jovial wave, shooing me away. So, I left him, splayed out on his couch in that big, dark apartment, alone with his unspeakable, urgent dreams.

"I'll see you tomorrow," I said, trying for a tenderness he could understand.

"You will," he answered as I shut the door.

• • •

The weather dipped. I wore a jacket for that long walk to and from the gym, my muscles tight from the cold. Stephen couldn't spar for at least a week, and Elvis and Kenny weren't around that Saturday when I met up with Danny at the gym. Stephen's roommate, Ed, towered over me as Danny explained that we'd fight each other today. As we wrapped and cupped and velcroed into our gear, I smelled his nervousness, inhaled it like a stimulant.

When the bell rang, he looked jumpy. I did what Danny taught me: in and out, hit and move. I rolled Ed's big haymakers, I bapped him lightly about the head. "Go for the body, Tommy!" Danny yelled. Ed looked at Danny, betrayed, but he wasn't the one training for a fight. I pulled my punches, but got in a few shots to the ribs. Despite his inches, I felt like the bigger man. *This is what winning feels like,* I thought, exultant, until I saw Ed's hangdog look.

A legitimate target.

I calmed myself, ashamed. Just as better boxers had instructed me, I told him as we pulled off our headgear and drank some water, "You're not bringing your hands back up to your face." Critique after sparring was considered a gift, a kindness not often offered and always appreciated. "And you're standing for too long without moving. Just be sure to move after you throw a punch if it doesn't land. If it does, keep hitting until you can't anymore."

Ed nodded, and we touched gloves. "Your reach is amazing," I added. "One straight right, and you could knock me right out." I didn't tell him to believe in his punches. I didn't know him well enough for that.

"I'm working on it," he said, and then Danny told us to go again, and Ed landed a nice clean right to the center of my forehead that knocked me backward, then got in a sweet combo at the bell.

"Good one, Ed!" Danny shouted, and I nodded my agreement. I knew what Ed felt like. After our last round, I hugged his bony body briefly, then got back in the ring with Danny.

"Now, again," Danny said through his gloves, calling me forward.

Late that night, I hit the pads on Danny's hands, hit his body suit, and he backed up dramatically as if I were doing some real damage. It struck me that men had to learn how to be touched again, and how to touch one another. I watched him wheeling over and thought it was generous, selfless even, for a champion boxer to be so ego-less as to give a guy back his dignity.

• • •

Increasingly, I saw my hope to build a bridge between my Before and After as a kind of binary of its own. I hadn't crossed a magical line as much as I'd exploded my life, creating change in the messy way most people do. That was the hardest truth. I had changed, and I had stayed the same, and it was up to me to learn how to build a new self with the materials before me. "We had the same socialization," I'd plead to Jess. "I am not that different than you." We knew it to be true, yet—it wasn't true anymore, not exactly.

Sometimes it felt as if she knew me better than anyone else ever had, like lifetimes of knowing, yet one lifetime she didn't know and couldn't understand. When she saw me, she saw Thomas and only Thomas. When we were upset with each other, to see my muscle and beard through her eyes was a heavy burden.

Jess, who held me when I shook as loss dislodged my mom from me, my mom and the child she birthed, the me she knew for thirty years before she died.

Jess, who told me Mom came to her in dreams when she first died with messages for me, who turned back toward me and put her head on my chest, who listened, who touched me. Jess, whom I knew I would marry that first night, when she pulled the Lovers card out of my tarot deck and said, so quietly, almost to herself,

"Dammit." Jess, who knew it too. Jess, who watched me strip off all of my wet, animal things, whom I could stand before naked.

Jess, who found me beautiful.

It took me so long to realize that, for her, for this lifetime, this Thomas was enough.

• • •

My mom, a physicist, taught me that time was a dimension. As the fight drew close, I hit the bag and hit the bag and hit the bag until I was in a trance, my body present to all the bodies around me and all the bodies I'd been and known, and I finally found a rare and perfect peace there.

This feeling manifested in unexpected moments, such as when the guys who ran Church's pointedly blasted that terrible nineties song "Closing Time" at nine thirty each night. That song delivered me back to senior year, driving around in my Dodge Intrepid with my gay best friend, and then going to the all-ages gay club we'd dance at most Fridays. Pegasus ended the night with Donna Summer's "Last Dance," and at the gym I could feel within myself both an exhausted man, hitting a heavy bag, and a tired teen in a sweaty fervor, melting into a mass with the glittering queens and the khaki butches and the diesel twinks and the leather daddies.

AMATEUR

Thwack, thwack, thwack. The smell of sweat. Late-night radio on a long drive home. My mom's stomach, gurgling as I wrapped my small arms around her. *You have a golden core,* I heard her say, on a loop. Danny unlaced my gloves and smiled at me, our faces wet. So many people, touching me, making me human again. Sometimes I cried without knowing it. *Who knows,* I'd think. *Maybe Danny did too.*

Danny, Stephen, and I were the only people left at Church's on most nights when that song came on. The other guys would throw on sweatshirts and head home, and I'd limp to the locker room, alone but for the one dude outside mopping and hollering through the door, "Five minutes!" I'd strip naked then and turn toward the mirror above the sinks, taking in how my body looked without any additions or subtractions, a blur of tattooed color and skin and hair, and I would think that I really was a beautiful man—for the lives I'd lived, and not despite them.

What's Wrong with Losing?

"You look like a genius on the mitts," Danny said, as we sped into November. Though that wasn't really true, as the fight approached, it was easy to see that I was improving, even when I lost. It wasn't so much about landing more punches, or knowing how to dip—it was the choice I'd make, no matter how often I found myself cornered, to come back out swinging. It was learning a language that transcended winning or losing. I thought often about the day I sparred Eric. Getting back up from that mat was my initiation into a different kind of masculinity, one far more complex, less fragile, and more meaningful than I'd imagined.

Three weeks before the fight, Stephen was approaching fighting shape and though his naked aggression still freaked me out, I was ready to face him whenever Danny decided the time was right. For the moment, Danny had him square off with Kenny, who rolled under his punches amiably while I watched with admiration. I was so caught up in their dance that I didn't notice Chris, appearing in his usual getup, until he called Danny and me over to the tables where boxers threw their bags or kept their spare gloves and hand wraps. It was a brutally cold day, the first glimpse of winter, though the gym retained its rainforest humidity, sweat condensing on heavy bags and the hitting end of our gloves. It made everything slippery.

"Eric still hasn't hit his weight," Chris said quietly to Danny and me, his voice solemn and a little pleading. "Do you think you can come up?"

I looked at Danny, who shook his head emphatically. Bulking before a fight slowed you down, and my biggest advantage was speed. I would not bulk.

"Nope," he added for emphasis. "Not gonna happen."

"What do you weigh now?" Chris asked me.

I reddened. "One thirty-three."

"Shit." We stood in an uncomfortable stand-off. I waited it out, watching Stephen rush Kenny, and Kenny cooly slip underneath his brutish advances. The squeak of their shoes echoed a little symphony in my ears.

"We'll get him to one thirty-five on fight day, like we promised," Danny finally spoke first. It was our compromise, and one Danny arranged as soon as he became my coach. I'd shed five pounds of water weight in the last few months, so putting it back on was my part. Eric had to do his. "He'll drink water, don't worry about it." I'd never seen Danny this way, shoulders broadened, not standing down.

Eric had agreed, months ago, to lose those ten pounds to fight me. Chris had to be desperate to be here, asking. I worried out loud, after he'd left, that they'd call off our match.

Danny, unfazed, was holding my spit-slimed mouthguard. He washed it off with his water bottle and handed it to me to grip loosely in my gloved hand. He saw an advantage: "Let him lose a lot of weight right before a fight." Danny grinned. "Let's see how much energy he has then."

I nodded, but it was hard to think of my weight when I was increasingly preoccupied by the due date of my younger brother's son, fast approaching. It felt strangely out of the order of things for Brett to be the first of us to become a father, and on the other side of the country. When I first moved out west, over a decade ago, my mom had been devastated by the distance. Now I was back, and she was gone, and we were still scattered, without her to orbit around.

Danny swatted my butt and hopped in the ring with Stephen. "Tommy, watch," Danny said.

I could see that he was imitating my style, or the style he'd taught me, anyway—fast, in and out. When Stephen rushed him aggressively, Danny rolled out and nailed him. I could taste the world we'd created here, the sweat and rubber, but I was thinking about Oakland, and the man who mugged me so many years ago. I was thinking about my life Before, and what is taken from us that cannot be recovered. Sometimes Danny kept up his guard and spoke to me through it while Stephen whaled away at him: "See, Tommy, I'm not hurt. I'm watching. I'm looking for my opportunity."

It was beautiful to see that Danny was okay even as he was getting hit. I could see the whites of his eyes. He looked very, very calm, and it was clearly driving Stephen nuts. Danny blocked every punch, rolled under a hook, then hit Stephen relentlessly, driving him to the ropes before laying off just short of the bell.

Danny walked up to me, only slightly out of breath. Stephen hollered a primal yell into the air, half in jest, smiling as usual. He was covered in sweat.

"Do you get it?" Danny asked. "Guys like that, you use their own energy against them. He's going to pressure you until he learns to be scared of you. Let him come at you with all that force, let him run into the ropes. Once you've trapped him, come back twice as hard." I knew he meant Stephen, who jumped up and down in his corner, but I saw so many men lined up behind them, men who used their bodies as weapons outside the ring, men who used to scare me and did not anymore.

I looked at Stephen, watching him psych himself up in his animal way, trying not to appear wounded by Danny's accurate analysis of his psychology. Maybe it was a lesson for Stephen too. He wasn't fooling any of us.

"Closing Time" played like a siren song. My advantage wasn't being a beginner, I realized, pulling off my hand wraps. It was seeing, really seeing, that I wasn't the only one.

"You took a lot and didn't react," Danny said, which was a compliment.

Did I lose? Who knows? If boxing taught me anything, it was that losing and winning were decided by judges, split-second decisions, freeze-frames, and systems stacked for or against us before we were born. Luck wasn't luck. It was rarely even timing.

"A fighter fights himself," Danny said over and over, steady as a drumbeat. It reminded me of the three central conflicts of narrative, the ones I'd learned in high school English class: man against man; man against nature; man against himself.

The first two were only meaningful in the context of the last. Danny was right, I thought often, most especially when I was shadowboxing. I'd face the mirror or weave between orange cones on the floor, imagining another version of myself, the man I thought I was supposed to be, the man I was fighting, the man I was. I wasn't trying to beat him.

I was trying to save him.

• • •

So, less than two weeks before my fight, I boarded a plane to San Francisco. Danny didn't have to tell me that the plan was ill-advised for my boxing prospects. But my small family and I had faced a much bigger fight since Mom died than my upcoming match in Madison Square Garden, and so my sister, brother-in-law, Jess, and I flew to San Francisco to be there for my brother, whose son was about to be born, because he would be my mother's grandson, and because she could not.

I knew that even the prescribed sprints, ab work, and six-mile runs couldn't replace the six days of training I'd miss. Before, I would have made my apologies and focused on my goal. But the heart of the experiment boxing had become was to face questions that got me on the plane, like: What sort of man was I? Who was I fighting for?

Mike Tyson's disturbing parable of an autobiography, *Undisputed Truth*, was weirdly prescient reading for my flight out. It is a tragic text, a stomach-turning argument against the worst kind of masculinity and the machinations of the sport itself. He details the genesis of his boxing carer: a street fight at ten with the bully who killed his pet pigeon. That moment of cruelty, against a backdrop of a startlingly abusive home life, led him away from his first instinct—tenderness—to a life defined entirely by violence.

I grabbed a pen and marked the places he lost himself into a cartography I did not want to follow. "I wanted to be a villain," he wrote in one particularly sad passage. "The villain is always remembered, even when he doesn't outshine the hero. Even though the hero kills him, he makes the hero the hero."

Regardless of his posturing, what makes a villain a villain is that he is the hero of his own story. My interest in Tyson stemmed from his compulsive earnestness. He was a veritable scholar on toxic masculinity, and he was right: a winner does indeed need a loser, and violence, from war to racism to rape, requires a story about why the enemy deserves to be overpowered.

"If your humanity rests on someone else not being human, then there's no humanity," Niobe Way, the developmental psychologist, said. It's a shadow made visible. Once you see it, you see it everywhere. It is the story of violence.

And it's hard to overestimate the impact of that distorted logic on masculinity. Way told me a story that haunted me: In 2012, she met with the seventh-grade boys she worked with in Manhattan. It was the same week twenty-year-old Adam Lanza had killed his mother, then drove to an elementary school in Newtown, Connecticut, and murdered twenty students, six adults, and himself. I covered that shooting at the paper I worked for in Boston. I had been a man for less than a year.

"Tell me," Way said to the kids, "why did that boy kill so many people?"

A few volunteered that he was "crazy."

"But tell me why he's crazy," she said.

The students considered that for a moment.

"He was lonely," three twelve-year-old boys with beginners' minds told her, in chilling unison.

• • •

Just as my path to manhood had been obscured by the shadow of his father, my brother faced the worst model possible for how to bring up a son. His father was a charming sociopath with a lilting Southern accent and a fondness for shooting dogs with BB guns.

When we arrived at Brett's family's front door in Oakland, he was obviously scared. He was also excited, carrying everyone's bags up the stairs to his house, looking like my baby brother again for the first time since high school.

As Brett and his wife, Cristina, walked us by a preschool in Berkeley they wanted to send their child to, as Brett talked about their prenatal classes and showed us the books in the baby's room, I saw that my brother and I would be more than okay, that we were already better than the man who raised us. As if that weren't the point of the story. As if I weren't writing a book about fathers and sons.

"I felt this shame growing up," Brett told me once, years ago. "I remember sitting in the van with you guys when you told me what Dad did to you, and I felt dirty. I felt, 'That's my father,' one; and two, 'I'm his son.' I struggled with the fact that I was a guy. I think it's been a lifetime struggle."

I thought a lot about that struggle when Brett joined me on my long prefight runs through Oakland, and we talked about his upgraded home-security system, and how scared he was to be a parent without having any parents himself. I knew I was the eldest, and the closest thing to it, so I told him he would be an excellent dad, because I was sure of it.

I was reminded of the time we went to Napa for his birthday many years earlier, before I was on testosterone and before he'd met Cristina, when we both were young and living in San Francisco. I had looked up his astrological chart as we idled away the time between vineyards. I told him that he was a Cancer rising and started to read the description off my phone as we drank coffee near the French Laundry, surrounded by tourists despite the drizzle.

"What does that mean?" he asked, his aviators mirroring my face back to me.

"It says you're imaginative, and sensitive, and nurturing." He looked chiseled and young, a little out of place still, living in a city after so many years in wintry industrial towns. I could see, in the months since he'd arrived, that he was becoming himself.

"I'm nurturing!" he echoed, his thick arms crossed across his chest. "I'm nurturing."

Since my transition, I've revisited that moment: my surprise at his enthusiasm, the emphatic way he announced it, the pride in his voice. What a reward it must have seemed to him to be acknowledged for the man he was, not the one he was afraid of becoming. Here he was, the person he'd been all along.

As we ran past my old haunts and his new ones, I could see our shadows along the gym and the bookstore and the coffee shop I'd once frequented on Rockridge Avenue. The Before me was nowhere and also everywhere, a paradox. Like gender. Like life.

"I'm nurturing," Brett had said, shaking his head. "Did you know that about me?"

We were leaning against a car, the two realest men you know, and of course I said yes.

. . .

I still failed sometimes too at being the man I wanted to be. Like when we were outside the grocery store and Brett asked me about the mechanics of throwing a hook after a straight right, and Clare—who had been taking boxing classes for years—tried to pipe in, and we both kept talking as if she didn't exist.

Clare, a tattooed social worker who regularly faced down clients who threatened to kill her, was a powerful presence, yet she was silenced by our jocular camaraderie so swiftly I didn't even notice that it had happened.

Jess pointed it out, gently, later that night. As soon as she mentioned it, I was transported back to the leafy sidewalk, Clare's voice behind us: "It's in the pivot—" she'd started to say. We were ten months apart and we'd been close our entire lives. I thought of Larissa. I couldn't believe I'd made the same sexist mistake again.

"You should just acknowledge it," Jess said, before falling asleep. I lay awake, hearing Clare speak, that small moment like a cresting wave, interrupted. How could I not notice my own sister's voice, clear and confident, then quashed, so quickly, by our lower ones? My sister, whose temper as a kid was unrivaled, whom I'd put money on in any fistfight, whom I'd always admired for her passion and the way she could easily channel it into a righteous and powerful rage.

As I considered how to apologize, I realized that a gulf between us had grown, glacially but steadily, since Mom's death. I knew that Mom had only allowed Clare to see her naked body, to help her use the toilet, to bathe. When she died, Clare had, overnight, become the only woman in our tiny family. At breakfast the next morning, I saw in the way she held herself and the questions she asked that she was trying to do for Brett what Mom would have, if she were here, and I smiled at her in a way that I hoped showed that I noticed.

Meanwhile, my nephew still hadn't arrived. We went on long walks and picked up vitamins and tried to distract Cristina from her discomfort. Our tickets home were prepurchased, but I considered extending our stay anyway, caught between worlds. Danny eventually texted me: I had to get back to training. It was a week before the fight. Did I want to get killed?

I knew he was right. Maybe it was stupid to fly across the country, to let my muscles weaken and my cardio fall apart, so close to fight night. Maybe I was making up for my guilt for all the Christmases and Thanksgivings I'd not come home for, not realizing until the last holiday we were together that Mom was really sick, and even then I had no idea that she would die within months. Being in Oakland was a messy reminder, as family always is, of my worst and best selves, the physics of my present and my past, running concurrent in collapsed time.

My siblings and I had always protected each other the best we could, but we couldn't fight each others' fights. I knew they would understand.

The next morning Jess and I left for home, missing Ronin's birth by just a day. I hugged my sister extra hard, making my body a bookmark, because I did not yet have the words that held both our history and our future, or an apology that acknowledged that the gravity between us had shifted in subtle, powerful ways.

On the plane ride home, thinking of her, I underlined a surprisingly poignant piece of advice that Cus D'Amato gave Tyson when he was sixteen, after he lost his first tournament fight: "You have to face your demons, Mike, or they will follow you to eternity. Remember to always be careful how you fight your fights, because the way you fight your fights will be the way you live your life."

I knew that Clare and I had lost something in my becoming, that my being a man changed everything, even the things I most wanted to stay the same.

My sister had been my best friend since I could remember, and I was humbled to realize that I was a beginner in this part of my life as well. I needed to learn how to be her brother too.

• • •

After I returned from Oakland, in the week before the fight, I remembered with more immediacy my life in my other body. I did not "deserve" the open-sesame quality of this life any more than I "deserved" the "wrong bathrooms," or the stepfather who molested me.

Nobody at the gym talked about politics, despite the brewing turbulence happening beyond its doors. No one talked about Clinton's emails or Trump's Twitter account.

Danny said he didn't care that the guys he trained were rich, that they were boxing for the thrill of it. He didn't care that I had no idea what I was doing, that I was a tourist, and a white one at that. "I don't think about it," he said, even when I pushed him. "You're all fighters to me."

But I thought about our different New Yorks as the fight drew near, and how they were laid over each other, and how Danny worked harder than me for longer, and his reward was being my coach and my reward was getting all the glory I could barely appreciate. I thought about being a white man in America. I thought about my pay raises, the assumptions of competency, the sudden freedom to walk alone at night, the way my body had transitioned from threatened to threat. I thought about the advantages thrown at me for an aesthetic that looked like a birthright. I thought about passing, and how it erased a part of me, and how hormones responded to context, and how race and masculinity were inventions that benefited me, and what I could do to challenge that.

"You have it in you," Danny said, as if he could hear my thoughts, though he was talking about the fight. "I just have to bring it out in you." He'd treated me differently since I'd come back from San Francisco: following me on my social media accounts, "liking" various photos and stories I shared. He hugged me longer at the end of every round, and he gave me meaningful looks over the top of his mitts.

"I see everything," he said. "Go again."

• • •

A tough blow: Chris came by a few days before the match to say that Eric had stopped showing up to training and that no one had heard from him, not even his coach. If I'm honest, a small part of me—the scared part—liked the out.

"Let it go," Danny said. "We have work to do."

Two days before fight night, I showed up at the gym and suited up as Danny announced my final challenge: a brutal day of "hard sparring" with Stephen, whose ankle had fully healed. Tomorrow would be easy: eating, bullshitting, watching fights on YouTube, Danny said. But today, punches would not be pulled. There would be no getting tired.

I nodded. Stephen looked at me with what I recognized as the desperation of a man with something to prove. But in the split second between when we jumped in the ring and the clear sound of the bell, I felt a calm stillness, as if I were a big fish at the bottom of the ocean. I thought it was adrenaline washing over me as he rushed me, but it wasn't: it was relief.

Time slowed. I met him in the middle of the ring, exchanged, got out. I stood my ground, didn't get pushed backward, didn't gas out. I worked the indented bite of my mouthguard like a baby chewing on a pacifier. I noticed every detail: The sound of my glove, connecting with his headgear. The bloom of pain in my gut as he pummeled my stomach. The arrhythmic heartbeat sounds of the others, pounding heavy bags and speed bags, all of us resting as the bell signaled the end of a round, each of us alone in our pursuit of glory but part of a larger organism, confined by time and starting over again and again. Stephen was brutal, even mean, but he never succeeded in intimidating me. I could see who he was, see the child he'd been, see the need and fear and beauty of his body, just like my own.

Stephen hugged me at the end of the last round. "You believed in your punches!" he said, grinning.

But the final test was yet to come. I shouldn't have

been surprised, but I was when Danny hopped in next and came at me harder than he ever had before. He didn't telegraph his big right, didn't ape Eric so blatantly. I'd gotten comfortable moving with him, but this wasn't our usual routine. He chased me around the ring, my mind gauzy with a very old betrayal.

"Keep your guard up!" Danny yelled. "Get off the ropes!"

I obeyed, awed a bit by Danny's hard hooks, the bruises forming on my face. He was merciless, and I could feel my energy draining as he stared right through me, not breaking character. He let up a little, crossing back to his side of the ring, eying me as the clock wound down.

"Come on, Tommy," he said, sounding like himself. "Do not gas out!"

I thought of all the ways I'd chosen to live, even when it felt impossible to be alive in this body, and I hit Danny, hard, in the stomach.

He sucked in air and nodded. We touched gloves so I understood that he wanted me to hurt him. "Don't hold back," he said.

Stephen hopped back in. I let him rush me the way Danny had showed me, and I stayed calm, breathed deep, and touched into a warmth deep in my chest. I fanned it, a controlled growing flame. Then I rolled, and rolled again, and rolled again. I could see Stephen getting tired, and that's when I hit him—he was slower to dodge my punches, and I got him good a few times around the head. I saw his head move in slow motion, saw his mistakes, got him with a hook and a cross.

Danny hollered with joy from the corner. Stephen, meanwhile, whooped when I punched him so hard his head spun, and I saw caution in his next approach.

I watched Stephen change into the fighter he wanted to be, I watched him come back harder. He only wanted to hurt me, I realized, because I'd asked him to.

I felt my cheeks bruising and put my arms up, just as I had when I sparred Eric that day two months earlier. This time, I knew how to hit back. I didn't want to, but I had to. Stephen looked at me like a man possessed, and I kept my gloves up. I counterpunched, I took on his energy as in physics, and I hit him as he hit me, but I never forgot his body was soft and pliable, like mine.

"You're ready," Danny said, at the bell, ecstatic. "You see that? You won all three rounds."

"You quit thinking," Stephen said approvingly, hanging off the ropes.

He was right, in his way. I had always kept my distance with men, like an animal on the perimeter of the herd. As I pulled off my gloves and packed up for the night, it occurred to me that what I had wanted, most of all, was to experience the rites and rituals of a manhood where violence could be managed, so that I could finally move beyond it.

So it happened that there I was, still intact, loving those men even as I hit them in the face, and knowing that they loved me back.

• • •

I called my sister that night. "I'm sorry," I began, and we talked about that day in Oakland, how I'd spoken over her, how I hadn't meant that moment to be gendered, and how I saw that it was. In this new life, I didn't realize that qualities that defined me positively in old dynamics didn't always translate well to new ones.

"Sometimes when I'm with both you and Brett, there will be just little moments where I'm the only female voice in the conversation," Clare said, "and that appears to not be valued in the same way—and neither of you appear to be aware of it at all."

I told her what I'd witnessed: That when Mom was dying, Clare had been the one to take family leave from work and brush Mom's hair and paint her nails so that she could exist in her body, even as it poisoned her. Clare had done the hard, dirty work of being present for my mom, who only showed herself in this way to her daughter. As I met with lawyers and funeral directors, my sister had been the dutiful daughter, just as our mother had done for her mother, and that, more than anything, was what I was sorry for.

What I didn't say was that I didn't know regret

until our mother was dying. I wish, more than anything else, that I had found the tenderness to hold her close, to tell her who I was, to insist as bravely as Clare did in bearing witness to her death. I let gender be an excuse because Mom seemed to want me to, because it was expected, because men often do. I wish I hadn't.

Clare forgave me—she even understood.

"Sometimes I worry that the old me is gone," I ventured, afraid of how she'd respond.

"You've grown and changed. You have done a lot more work to be more emotionally present, to listen more, to be more open to suggestion. But it's not like that person is lost."

I lingered with her on the phone. I hadn't let myself imagine that the women in my life might think I was a better person for becoming the man I am.

"I miss you," I told her. I had pictures of holding her when she was born, my hair short, with me already insisting on pants. Growing up, she had the She-Ra castle, and I the He-Man one, and we played together in our way, beyond gender, with our dolls. She had understood my body, my place in the world, before either of us had a language for it.

Love for myself allowed me to stick a needle deep in my thigh every week. I'd not always remembered the people who still, every day, taught me how to believe in a world that was good, and forgiving, and beautiful, and that they needed me as much as I needed them.

Clare said that she was grateful that I was her sibling, in all my incarnations. "I had the privilege of growing up in a family where gender wasn't necessarily taken for granted by everybody," Clare said. "It really forced me to be, like, 'Who am I?'"

Among the many answers, there was one we both knew for sure: she was my sister, and I her big brother—the only one.

• • •

"The definition of masculinity, whether you are 'for it' or 'against it,' is that it's one-size-fits-all, and it's bad: Violent, testosterone-driven, predatory," Michael Kimmel, the masculinities studies professor, told me once. "I don't think that's true. The biggest misconception is that there's one definition of masculinity and everybody subscribes to it."

Deconstructing the man box and the harm it causes every body, male, female, and otherwise, begins with challenging that idea and offering, in its place, the reality of our actual bodies. To build equitable relationships and societies, to create a world free of unwanted violence, to tackle the masculinity crisis—we must first acknowledge how we each are failing, right now, to see the full spectrum of humanity in ourselves and in others.

The next day, I found myself thinking about all the ways I'd let others' ideas of manhood shape me: the embarrassment of others when I cried, or the nods of approval when I said, "Yeah, I box," the admiration for this black eye, this bruiser body, this silence in the year since my mom died, this "being so brave," this "doing so well" in "acting so strong."

Eating banh mis with the guys at a punk-rock Vietnamese dinner spot, I listened to Stephen talk about smoking cigars on a beach somewhere when this whole thing was over and noticed the look softening Danny's face. "I'm really going to miss you guys," he said. "We're like family."

Family, like gender, is contextual. Boxing didn't make me more of a man. But, sitting across from Danny, I knew I was a better man for having met him.

These men had taught me how to love, with clearer eyes, the beautiful paradoxes I found in masculinity, the way it could hold a bloody nose and a hug, a sharp razor on the jaw under the tender watch of a barber, the muscle that must be carefully nursed to its potential, the body that could make a puppy or a child feel sheltered, cocooned.

Stephen would soon go back to Wall Street, Danny to supplementing his income by training women from the Upper East Side looking to mix up their cardio, and I to being the guy NPR called to comment on trans media visibility. But here, in these last days, no matter how minor our impending glory and how huge the divides of our daily lives, we had reached a transcendence, if only in passing.

"The test of a first-rate intelligence," F. Scott Fitzgerald famously wrote, "is the ability to hold two opposed ideas in mind at the same time and still retain the ability to function."

Boxing was the beginning of a path, not a means to an end. That I knew for sure.

Danny interrupted my thoughts. "You got balls to do this, you know?" He sat across from me, then said it again, looking me straight in the eyes. Over noodles, my stomach yellowing with bruises, I nodded my thanks, understanding that my not, in fact, having balls didn't matter to anyone anymore, least of all me.

●　●　●

Backstage at the Garden, coaches had shed their hoodies and Nikes for shiny shoes, collared shirts, and sweaters. They were reverent, watching us like nurses bedside checking a patient's color, on the lookout for anything out of the ordinary: too much bravado from a quiet type, somatic complaints, telltale nervous tics, stooped shoulders. All us fighters gathered in our regulation shorts and tanks, and those of us who worried we'd showed up light took advantage of the snack platter while we waited to be weighed.

"Not a second goes by that he's not eating," Chris said to Danny, who looked uncomfortable in his dress pants and sharp gray sweater. The queasy energy of the gathering group was making me jumpy, so Danny and I hung out in a bunkerlike hall away from the others, fighters and their coaches brushing by us as they made their way between the weight and changing rooms. I took Chris seriously, inhaling two liters of water, two peanut-butter sandwiches, and two bananas in thirty minutes.

At weigh-in, I stripped down to the roomy boxers I'd bought just for this occasion.

"One thirty-five point four," the ancient USA Boxing official called out.

I did it, I thought. The goal had been to get as close to 140 as possible, and to at least hit 135. Somehow, I'd followed through on every impossible promise I'd made.

"You're prepared mentally," Danny said, as the doctor listened to my heart and then handed me the pen to sign the waiver. I saw the words but didn't need to read them, knowing them, understanding them, *trauma* and *death*. These words had brought me here, and this was the language in which I could, finally, face them.

Chris pulled Danny and me into the hallway and said the refs had agreed to let Eric and me fight no matter the weight differential, as long as he showed up. He was an hour late. Danny had offered to fight me instead, "like an exhibition," but the officials said no.

"No matter the weight differential". was an unusual ruling. Professional boxers weigh in the day before a bout, famously starving and sweating themselves as light as possible, then gaining multiple pounds back in the hours before the match. The thinking is that it's easier to shed water and then put it back on, while going up a weight class means having to add power along with weight.

Assuming Eric showed up heavy, the biggest danger was getting knocked out. But that wouldn't be the worst failure, and neither would losing—it would be, on this very last occasion, not fighting at all.

I waited Eric out in the changing room with Kenny, Stephen, and some other guys. The tone was strangely grim. Stephen seemed especially subdued, huddled into himself, watching fight videos on his phone.

To keep me busy, Danny asked an old-timer to wrap my hands with the regulation gauze and pads. This special technique is meant to better protect a fighter's hands from boxer's fracture, and the production took a good fifteen minutes.

Most people don't realize that boxing gloves are

weapons. You train and spar with sixteen-ounce gloves, which look and feel like marshmallows and do the least amount of damage to your hands and the face of the guy who's helping you get better. But fight night requires the much-lighter twelve-ounce gloves, which are guaranteed to cause black eyes, bloody lips, and broken bones because they are socks for your fists, and your fist is a precise missile that you have trained to bloody and break things.

But I wasn't thinking about weaponry just then. I was thinking that, all day, men had taken care of me. I'd spent the afternoon at the barbershop, getting my hair cut by a new guy, who correctly read my mood and used his clippers in total silence. I relaxed into the chair, and when he put the hot towel across my eyes, I closed them.

"What do you do?" the old guy wrapping my hands asked. He touched me with such gentleness, I almost cried. "Writers are great fighters," he said when I told him, surprising me.

"Really?"

But he didn't have a chance to explain. "He's here," Danny said, returning from Eric's weigh-in. He was ninety minutes late. All the guys in the room cheered his arrival. "So it's happening!" I said, sweat already forming slick lines down my back. Stephen, in an open dress shirt, reached out and hugged me.

"What was his weight?" I asked Danny.

"I don't know," he said, which was clearly a lie, "but I'm not gonna tell you when I find out."

Eric, I learned much later, weighed in at 152.4 pounds.

• • •

In the ring, the fighter is entirely alone—without teammates, the rules upheld by a single referee, the match scored subjectively by three strangers. A fighter spends those rounds exposed: Blood drips from lips, eyes swell shut, arms grow weak and heavy. I was there, I understood, because I wanted all of me to be seen.

But I was there, also, because people helped me get there: the guys in my corner, my coach, my partner, my sister, my brother, my mother, my friends. I needed a lot of help, and my life changed when I learned how to ask for it.

"The number one shame trigger for men is being perceived as weak," shame researcher Brené Brown told *Redbook* in a 2012 interview. She described men who say they give their partners "enough" to be perceived as open, but hold back total honesty out of fear of being judged.

Of course men are weak, and sad, and lonely. We are lost, and unsure, and scared. And we are all the more those things for how hard they are to say.

I put in my mouthguard, the teeth marks perfectly matching my teeth. I boxed my shadow, which was also me. Stephen, perhaps troubled by the quiet, abruptly stood up on a chair and began reading a Tyson quote off his phone.

"'I'm afraid of losing,'" Stephen read in a strong, sure voice. "'I'm afraid of being humiliated.'"

I made brief eye contact with Danny, then we both watched Stephen because he needed us to.

"'But I was totally confident,'" he went on, his white dress shirt flapping, still open over his bare chest. He was more than one self at once too. "'The closer I get to the ring, the more confidence I get. The closer, the more confidence I get. The closer, the more confidence I get.'" It sounded, the way Stephen said it, like a prayer or a spell. I thought about Tyson's memoir. The most triumphant moment, the bravest he'd ever been, hadn't been in the ring, but the moment he decided to quit. That's the Mike Tyson story that never gets told. He fought because what he really wanted was to be loved. Plants will always grow toward the sun.

"'All through my training I've been afraid of this man,'" Stephen read, gaining steam, raising his arms in the air. I could picture him as a boy, gathering the other kids to him. "'I thought this man might be capable of beating me. I've dreamed of him beating me. I always stayed afraid of him.'"

Then Stephen paused. "'The closer I get to the ring, I'm more confident.'"

Outside the door, they called the guys for the sixth bout.

"'Once I'm in the ring,'" Stephen said, looking right at me, "'I'm a God! No one can beat me.'" He gave me a thumbs-up, this moment a gift in the way he knew to give it; then I wiped my eyes with my gloves, the little damp spots proof of a life beyond and within this one.

Then they called my name.

Why Do Men Fight?

Danny looked at me with raised eyebrows as the spotlights roamed the crowd. "You ready?" It wasn't really a question.

Just as on that last night of hard sparring, I felt my own hot breath, the muscles in my chest, the squeeze of my fists in my gloves. I was scared, and I was a fool, and I was ready—and so I jumped. That jackrabbity motion had driven Errol crazy in the beginning of my training, the being "light on my feet," a nervousness that never totally disappeared. I jumped up and down the whole way to the ring, my fist in the air, wanting to show myself the sheer force of my will, the will that pushed me to fight after only a few months of training, and the same will that kept me alive in the face of the men who had tried to destroy me.

I could hear the rumbling of the crowd, taking

notice. Danny laughed as the cheering grew louder. I hopped like a madman, up and down, my hands in the air, feeding off the crowd. Thousands of people hollered for me as I climbed into the ring, a wave of sound.

When I'd left the apartment, Jess did not tell me to be careful but wished me luck instead. It was a measure of adulthood, I thought, carrying my bag down the stairs, that no one was around anymore to worry over my body in the way a mother does. What a burden and a freedom to be the sole person in charge of my safety, to risk what I wanted of it, and to be trusted to survive.

I am not sure I've ever felt more fearless than I did hopping up and down to the fight song, approaching the ring in the center of Madison Square Garden. If something terrible happened to me, I thought, looking at the stretcher, I would not regret it.

Right before the bell rang, I looked out in the crowd for Jess and my sister and brother-in-law, who'd come in last minute from Boston to watch. I saw them, and the coworkers and friends who'd also bought tickets, off in the middle distance, far from the fat-cat ringside tables. I waved, hearing my name, and felt a shiver through the whole of my body, the whole of my life. Here I was, the man I was when I stopped being afraid of the man I was becoming.

• • •

The fight was set for three rounds of three minutes each, with one-minute rest breaks in between.

Eleven minutes can be a very long time. Someone in the world, right now, will use the next eleven minutes to have sex, cook dinner, end a relationship or start one. Eleven minutes is long enough to fire someone, conduct a civil marriage ceremony, and for just about anyone to run a mile. An eleven-minute death would be excruciating to witness. My first testosterone shot, injected by a nurse-practitioner in Boston, took approximately eleven minutes, including teaching time. It was the time, in total, between when my mugger tackled me in Oakland, held a gun to my head, and let me live. In 2009, French free diver Stéphane Mifsud held his breath underwater for an unfathomable eleven minutes and thirty-five seconds. Eleven minutes can destroy civilizations.

At the bell, I leaped toward Eric and hit him with a jab just as he counterpunched over it. But I got in a few other nasty head shots before moving out of his range, and that first, crucial exchange was mine. That was the plan, to take him in round one, to let him know that the man he'd sparred two months ago was gone, and to introduce him to who was standing in his wake.

Eric, meanwhile, mostly stood still, watching me curiously as I charged in, hit, and got out. To come forward, I found I had to marshal up every reason I could think of to hit him in the face: that illegal hold when we sparred, the face he made when he looked at me, his being late, and heavy, and the entitlement and the sneering and the bad sportsmanship.

He moved slowly, barely keeping his gloves up as I punched through them. The crowd's cheers grew louder, in that primal way of people who smell blood. I hit him but eventually I was not hitting him. I was hitting my stepfather, and the doctors who didn't tell me how sick Mom really was, and the surgeon who said curtly that Mom didn't qualify for the lifesaving liver transplant, and the nurses who ignored her cries of pain at the Medicaid nursing home until we forced them to send her to the ICU, and she was right that she had to go, because she was dying. I hit him for the months after, the silence, the way I'd hid from her photos because remembering that she was dead did, in fact, feel like getting punched in the face.

I hit him four times for every haymaker he tried to land. I hit him because I wanted to show him that I would not be intimidated by his weight, or strength, or boyhood, or the way he'd nearly taken my head off when we sparred. I hit him to prove something to my own worst self, my shadow.

And, for a brief moment, I was eclipsed by it.

I could feel Eric's pride tanking as he tried and failed to pressure me, to lean into my punches, to get me on my heels. I was a blur, coming in with dozens of blitzes and pushing him back, back, back, until all he could do was cover his face, cornered, and the bald referee had to separate us. He turned toward Eric, hand out: One, two, three, four—

I put my gloves in the air and danced around Eric, like a real asshole. I was the sweat dripping off my arms, the goose bumps on my legs, the hardening of the muscles in my jaw, the light on my face, the swelling of my lip, the force of my will, the fact that I was not dead.

The referee quit counting and motioned Eric toward the center of the ring, a gesture that said, *Start fighting back or this is over.* Eric obeyed, coming out of the corner and cracking through my guard a few times with that vicious right, but I kept hitting and hitting. I sweated and panted from the clean effort of outscoring him, fair and square. As a ring attendant pounded out the gavel that indicated the ten-second mark, Eric threw himself into me, and I hit him with another combination that knocked him back into the ropes.

The bell rang, high and sweet, and I returned to my corner, my body nearly collapsing against Danny's.

"There we fucking go," Danny said. "That was beautiful. We're in his fucking head." Danny pushed me by my shoulders down onto a stool in the ring and poured a bottle of water over me. "We need to be in his head. See how fucking tired he is mentally? We got this fight." Danny studied me. "Don't show that you're tired."

I could feel my head ballooning with pain, my eyes squinting closed, my rage dissipating.

All my life, men have hurt me. It wasn't noble, but the worst part of me wanted to learn how to hurt them back.

If I'd begun boxing to face the shadow of the man I could be, then I was really facing him now: I knew I was capable of violence, just like anybody else. What did I want to do with it?

• • •

Eric's eyes, dead all of round one, were bright again. Whatever his coach had said to him, whatever hot shame or righteousness had been stoked in the sixty seconds between rounds, he was a different man. He didn't look lethargic, or defeated, or even defiant.

He looked pissed.

As I charged forward, he stuck out his right glove and gestured like *Come and get it.* The crowd erupted.

I tried to rush him, but he didn't let my punches push him back. He held steady, his big body harder than mine, and swung back. He hit me so hard, my headgear pitched to the side.

He wouldn't be chased around anymore. I watched his chest grow broader as the hits to my head slowed me

174

down. My guard slipped a few times, and he punched right through it.

Meanwhile, I could hear a growing chant: "Eric! Eric! Eric!" The improbable victor, just as he'd hoped. I was the villain of his story.

He pressed me into a corner. I got out from under him, but was on my back legs. He chased me around the ring, throwing as he moved, and I forgot to stand still and just hit back. He had me against the ropes, covering my face, when the ref pulled him off me, his eyes wild with rage.

I got a standing eight. I could smell the acrid sweat of my gloves as I adjusted my headgear, waving off the ref, just as I did that first time we sparred: *I'm fine I'm fine I'm fine.*

• • •

In the final round, we both wheezed and wobbled, staring at each other. The crowd was growing tired too. In eleven minutes, we had both won and lost.

I didn't hate him, that was the problem.

It was a peaceful feeling. The fight was coming to a close. I wondered if this was what death felt like, just the labored sound of my own breathing. I hoped so, because I was not afraid, or resigned. *Present,* I thought.

Eric pressed me into my corner, punching me hard in the head until the ref pulled him off. The crowd made O's with their mouths, laughing and cheering as they held their beers. I was not angry at them, as I thought about our shared yearning and bad breath and black eyes and missed chances and resentments and silk robes.

I saw my mom, cheering me as she once had my brother at his ice-hockey games. I understood, in that moment, her hallucinations near the end. I forgave her for thinking my brother was me, for not knowing how to say good-bye, for dying. I forgave myself too.

Eric stalked the ring, watching, hungry for that knockout.

"Eric, Eric, Eric!" people yelled.

He nailed me so hard, my head turned a strange angle.

"Always hit back twice as hard," Danny would say, so I threw a straight right. He ducked, but I got him with a jab that knocked him on his heels. I was dizzy, uneven on my feet, but I tried to come in again anyway. He nailed me in the chin and I cursed as my head popped back. We lumbered around each other, throwing wild jabs. *Come on,* I willed my body, but not before he got in another straight right, and another. I jabbed back. *Come on.* He hit me again.

I was still standing, at least.

I could feel the ring beneath my feet and the sweat in my hair as the bell rang. I turned around and walked back to my corner, my eyes already black. I high-fived Danny and smiled big for the JumboTron.

I won.

• • •

Except, I didn't.

In the center of the ring, the announcer held our gloves, as we faced the crowd, and said, "All three judges scored this match identically. Your winner, fighting out of the blue corner—"

As he raised Eric's glove, Eric's face sagged into a relief that softened me.

I turned to hug him, our arms sliding briefly around each other's beaten bodies, and I felt, in the flushing of the violence that I'd done and had been done to me, that I wasn't hugging him, but a lost part of myself.

One Week Later

"So how come you didn't tell me?" Danny said in a cut-the-bullshit voice. We were in a sterile coffee shop around the corner from Church's. I'd called him to meet up after my black eyes healed, telling myself I wanted to interview him, or thank him. But a tension was knotting my stomach, coiled under the surface.

The day after the fight, I woke up to a photo Danny had posted on Instagram of the two of us. We were in the ring a couple of hours before the match, arms around each other's shoulders, just as they were setting up the stretcher. He'd written, "With everything against us, Thomas showed me it takes more than a 20-pound disadvantage to slow us down. His heart is unquestionable. The average man wouldn't do what he's done."

I was touched, and struck, by the language: *the average man.*

I'd begun the interview professionally, asking him all the requisite background questions, and he'd humored me: he told me about being overweight as a kid, and the older sister who got him into boxing. I held my swiftly chilling coffee in my hand, and Danny picked at his sandwich, and our conversation devolved into small talk, so eventually I cut the recorder and stood up to go.

Danny looked at me for a long time, still sitting.

I sat back down. "Yeah?"

"So how come you didn't tell me?"

I studied Danny's face. It reminded me of Jess, that night on the dance floor, how she knew our future before I did, how she was not scared to meet me in exactly the place where I was.

"I figured this was why you wanted to interview me in the first place." He shrugged, messing around with the sandwich wrapper, and I held my breath as he told me that he'd figured out I was trans the week of my fight, noticed the word on my Instagram. "I knew what it meant, but I didn't know what it *meant*."

We looked at each other for a long moment.

"Can I record this?"

He nodded.

• • •

Testosterone activates genes, creating a twin of your-self. When I first injected a needle into my thigh, I did not know if I would go bald, or if my voice would get low, or how hairy I'd become. I knew I'd never be tall or have sperm, but whether I'd be able to grow a beard was up in the air. It is easy for people to see a man like me and think, *Trans men are men too*. But not all trans men look like me.

In the cold light of the postfight drudgery, seeing the photo Danny had posted, I felt conflicted. Sure, I'd wanted to report back from the most brutally mascu-line environment I could think of without the risk that guys would censor themselves or treat me differently.

What would have changed if the guys had known, all along, that I was trans?

I felt what shame researcher Brené Brown calls "the fear of disconnection."

This was the root of my personal crisis of mascu-linity, I realized. A part of me feared, still, no matter how dumb and toxic I knew it was, that I wasn't "real" enough. Whatever Danny said, I told myself, I would not let it define me.

Still, I braced myself, fearing that his reaction could undo me. His faith in me in this form, so soon after I lost my mom, had felt parental.

"I figured the reason that you didn't want me to

know was because it was in a boxing gym and you didn't want that type of attention," he said, clearly still stung. "It shocked me—I had no idea, nobody knows, nobody would have known—nobody still knows. It's shocking to know that you kept it in."

I nodded. It was shocking, he was right. Just as I hadn't believed, really believed, that I could be a man and be loved outside the ring, I hadn't thought I could be my whole self and be loved within it.

"Trust me, during the fight, it was in my mind," he said.

I pulled my napkin into tiny pieces under the table, still not sure what he was getting at.

"I was, like, 'Oh, man, this is going to be the best thing ever,' " he finally said. "I was thinking, 'If this guy fucking wins, oh my God.' "

We grinned at each other.

"I was just waiting for you to tell me," he said.

• • •

In W. C. Heinz's book *The Professional*, a reporter says to a boxer, "The rest of us have to prove our manliness, or something, by standing up to some guy. A fighter never has that urge because he gets rid of it in his work. That's why I say that, when everything else is equal, fighters are the best-adjusted males in the world."

To which the boxer replies doubtfully, "I don't know."

I don't know either. It's a paradox.

Boxing breaks many of the binaries that men are conditioned to believe about our bodies, our genders, ourselves. With its cover of "realness" and violence, it provides room for what so many men lack: tenderness, and touch, and vulnerability. The narratives we see about boxing matches always start at the ending: two guys in the ring, squaring off. The violence obscures the deeper story, the one about the fighters who see your biggest weakness and teach you how to turn it into an advantage. In gyms all over the world, men are sharing their worst fears, men are asking for help, men are sparring one another with great care.

In my five months boxing, I saw men weep unself-consciously. Over and over, men tied and untied my headgear and cup and gloves. An amateur fighter I did not know spent an hour one day at the gym giving me a pep talk, dotted with his own failings, after watching me get clobbered by Stephen—Stephen, whom I continued to see around the neighborhood with his comically large hunting dog, no less kind to me outside the ring or after he learned I was trans.

"I'm the guy that's sitting at the corner with the dogs smoking cigars with the MTA workers who are supposed to be downstairs working, but they're just blowing off steam," he once told me, about his place in the universe. "Tomorrow, I'm the guy who's hanging out with some starving artist, and then next week some successful artist, and then the next day some big Wall Street hotshot, then hanging out with the super of my building. I have a lot of masculinity models. I try to observe and take the best features of different types and combine them."

He wasn't the man I thought he was, but then again, I wasn't the man he thought I was either.

"It was unfortunate that the fight turned out the way it did with us," Danny said over his wilting sandwich. "But you did fucking excellent. I don't regret anything."

"It was a good fight, and I lost it," I said, breaking a cardinal rule of boxing.

Danny looked as if he were going to argue, but he didn't. He wasn't the average man either, and we both knew that I was right.

"I would never have treated you differently," Danny told me. "There's nothing different about you, or anybody that's trans. Nothing different," he said, just like he'd said that I had balls that night before the fight, when he knew that I, in fact, didn't. "There's no gender—it's all in your head. You performed as well as any other man would."

"I had to prove it to myself." I knew as I said it that it was true.

"Well"—he threw away his trash and pushed open

the door to the coffee shop, the sun, strangely bright for a bleak November day, rendering him backlit—"you proved it to me."

His face was visible once again: my friend, Danny. He held the door for me, like, *You coming?*

I wanted this to be a story about men and violence that didn't end with *That's just how guys are*, but until I lived it, I did not believe that it was possible.

Danny gestured again, *Come on*. I stood in his shadow for just a moment and then I stepped after him, into the light.

EPILOGUE
2017

As my own masculinity crisis stabilized, America's took an explosive turn. The rumbling energy on Orchard Street that day was now on the surface, exposed, and the whole country faced the violent fallout.

As for me, I still failed a lot: at not interrupting, at giving enough of myself when people were in need, at listening to feedback, at listening in general. But I also remembered that change starts with paying attention. I never stopped benefiting from my body in space: the silence when I speak remains, as does my ability to walk alone down dark streets at night without fear. But it grew ever easier to disavow the parts of manhood that troubled me. I dropped my towel in locker rooms, knowing that I could claim my male body, with all of its history, as enough.

I just had to fight for it.

I learned how to come forward from Danny, but I quit boxing that night in Madison Square Garden. My fight came out in new ways, like in the otherwise ordinary business meeting after the unmasking of Hollywood executive Harvey Weinstein, when a brusque colleague told me she had fended off men at work for years and had reported it each time. We were alone, and when I told her I was sorry, the stories cascaded out. She said she'd been touched and propositioned, that she actually thought it was normal, even as she knew it wasn't. She said she didn't even believe herself.

"I believe you," I said. I could feel, in the electric air, that those words meant something very different in this body.

"I believe you," I said, over and over, to Jess, to my friends, to my coworkers, and especially in front of other men. I believed women had been abused, raped, underpaid, passed over for promotions, shut down, and interrupted. I knew it as well as I knew myself.

I believed every story, and saying so became an incantation, a small but necessary beginning, a rebellion: it was something, I knew, that men were not "supposed" to do.

I thought of Danny, peeking out over his gloves.

"See, Tommy, I'm not hurt. I'm watching. I'm looking for my opportunity." Half of knowing how to fight is just being willing, really willing, to pay attention.

I saw everything.

• • •

Which is, in its own way, why I was in the desert dark of Palm Springs in my sensible rental, driving slow and steady into the night.

I carried a photo of a man my sister had found in an old photo album, an ex of my mother's who looked a lot like me: the same eyes, my sister and I agreed. He and I had exchanged emails and agreed to meet near his home in Joshua Tree, so I brought Mom in her urn and we flew across the whole of our divided country.

Jess was the first to suggest I try to meet the man who might be my biological father. She and I were newly engaged, and maybe she sensed in me the last unresolved shadow. It was the last thing I had to do before we married, the ending that allowed me a new beginning.

But it was my mother who got me on the plane. Before I knew she was sick but shortly before she died, Mom asked me if I would consider having children. I'd always been skittish about the idea, but maybe she sensed that my transition had awakened in me new possibilities. She wanted me to pass on my genes, she said. The words hung between us for a beat, taking the fuzzy shape of the man who wasn't there, the man she always said was a one-night stand, and the limitations of my body: none of it a mistake, all of it out in the open.

"I can't have biological kids," I reminded her finally.

"Oh," she said, surprised. "I forgot." Maybe it was the illness talking, but I knew what she meant.

She told me, with an urgency that would only strike me later, that I should think about it, regardless. It was unlike her to belabor a point, and she'd not once mentioned wanting to be a grandmother, but her desire for me to have kids was, I recognized, a referendum on her own choice to have me.

"Having children is the best thing I ever did," she said. I believed her. I heard, in her voice, a letting go. I heard a good-bye.

• • •

After I woke up in the dry heat and did push-ups on the floor of my hotel; after I watched the sun bake the lifeless land and the jackrabbits hop across the alien landscape; after I arranged to meet my maybe-father the next morning at a coffee shop in town—I put on Mom's favorite Paul Simon album and cried.

I was there, I realized, to finally be alone with all my ghosts.

"You were my miracle baby," my mom once told

me. She was here with me, as I made terrible coffee. So was Stephen, his shirt flapping as he read that Tyson quote in the belly of Madison Square Garden, blessing me as I howled unself-consciously into a limp pillow.

"'All through my training I've been afraid of this man,'" he said. "'I thought this man might be capable of beating me. I've dreamed of him beating me. I always stayed afraid of him.'"

A fighter fights himself, I thought, as the sun set and the air finally cooled. I thought about the experts I'd spoken to in my hope for some bigger answer, people who shared with me their most urgent and personal questions in the hope of helping me face mine. I thought about Niobe Way, who, when I asked her how to be a "good man," suggested forgoing that question for bigger and better ones such as "What are you doing in your life that's actually keeping the status quo?" or "How are you keeping silent in terms of things you see?"

"What's a man?" Danny had said, the last time I saw him. We'd been in the back room of Church's, among a new batch of fighters hitting heavy bags, and he'd shoved his arms through the sleeves of his black hoodie, looking at me as if I already knew the answer, because I did. "I think there's no definition. I feel like it's just a category to be put in."

That night, as I sat on the trunk of my rental car in the desert, watching the dime-size moon rise, I was the only human body, male or otherwise, for miles in any direction. It was strange to think that this too was America, with its bugs buzzing and bats rustling in the distance.

My thoughts returned to the month before I began injecting testosterone, back at the beginning of the masculinity crisis. I'd driven up to Oregon from California to see my stepfather for the first time in a decade. This was before I went on testosterone, when I first suspected that facing my fears could provide answers, even uncomfortable ones. I was surprised by what I saw in his papery, scruffy face, his crumbling, old-man body. He did not scare me, and I did not hate him. His life seemed, suddenly and completely, a waste.

How am I keeping silent about the things I see?

For there to be "good men," there have to be bad ones.

As soon as I spotted my stepfather, old and alone, I stopped believing in monsters. When he waved goodbye to me on that chilly spring night, shuffling off down the street corner, I knew it would be the last conversation we ever had. In it, he'd told me that he too had been abused as a child.

I have only ever known one father, and I knew he was hoping for my forgiveness, but I couldn't find that quite yet. So I told him, in my Before body, that I was so sorry that it had happened to him.

He looked surprised, the difference between us so clear in that moment. I never forgot it because it felt like the foundation I could build a life on: despite everything, I believed that as long as he was alive, he could change.

I still do.

• • •

The desert night made spooky sounds, and the air felt electric with so much that I could not see in the dark. Soon, I would head inside and go to sleep on this strange bed and wake up to this same landscape, bathed in light. I thought about the Stanford race historian Allyson Hobbs, who had written the book on passing. She and I had spoken for hours, sharing a communion that spanned far beyond the materials of our work, searching for hope while not turning our eyes away from this America, now.

"The tide will turn, and then we'll move into another moment, and then that moment will have its own historical significance and historical particularities," she said. "That's what I say to my students, but in my own heart, I feel so pessimistic right now because I just feel that so much of what's happening is not—it really is unprecedented. How do you explain all of this?"

It's a paradox, to know we need a future that we can't yet imagine.

Like being a man, lying on the roof of my car in the desert, inhabiting the same skin I'd had back in high school. As a teenager, I often drove out to the old, abandoned airfield beyond the airport. I used these same eyes to watch the planes take off for hours, envisioning with this same brain the life I would someday live in New York, or Los Angeles, or Tokyo, confusing freedom with escaping the past.

But we need a clear-eyed sense of our history, even the ugly parts, because without it we are mindless actors in stories we never agreed to. I thought of my mom, and how she'd envisioned a life for me and then created it. I thought of the night I'd spent recently in Washington, DC, alone in her old stomping grounds. I'd wandered late one Saturday past the Washington Monument and the White House, Constitution Gardens and the monument for fallen soldiers, until I'd arrived at the Lincoln Memorial. I could see her, an aspiring scientist, full of potential as this country we share, watching Martin Luther King Jr. say that he had a dream that one day we would realize it.

I did not care if this man was my dad, I realized, on the roof of the car in the desert, because this was never a story about fathers. I am, and always will be, only ever my mother's son.

Just then, out in the desert, two coyotes—those

wounded-looking tricksters—ran past me, giving me a shiver. They paused and turned back, and sure, I was scared a little, but as we looked at one another I unbuttoned my shirt and faced whatever was to come, with my invented chest and arms wide-open.

Acknowledgment

My dear friend Emily Carlson's clear-eyed kindness and poetic sensibility in both life and writing enriched each draft of this book. My work here was sustained by her and other generous readers, among them Anisse Gross, Julie Greicius, Annie Mebane, and Lauren Morelli, who have each taught me so much about how to tell a better story, especially this one.

I am grateful to the editors I've worked with over the years, whose insights helped shape my writing here: Isaac Fitzgerald, Tyler Trykowski, Heather Landy, Indrani Sen, and especially Xana Antunes, who did a beautiful job editing the story I wrote for *Quartz*, "Why Men Fight," upon which this book is based. I am so thankful to everyone at *Quartz* for helping me hone these ideas, and allowed me the time and space to pursue them, especially Kevin Delaney, who greenlit the original boxing story, and Zach Seward, who could not have been a better boss.

I am indebted to the experts I spoke to who patiently and graciously engaged my "beginner's mind." Sarah Helweg DiMuccio, whose work with Danish men elegantly highlighted the incredible impact of cultural narratives on masculinity. Allyson Hobbs, whose thoughtful scholarship on racial passing gave me a much more visceral understanding of that subject, among many others. Many thanks to Michael Kimmel for his grounding, richly resourced perspective on masculinities, and his generosity in connecting me to his vast network. Nell Irvin Painter's work on whiteness was critical to this book, and I still find myself thinking most days about our conversation on race and masculinity, which truly changed how I saw everything. I am grateful to Robert Sapolsky and Barry Starr for helping me understand the ins and outs of testosterone. Caroline Simard's fascinating scholarship on unconscious bias was foundational to the chapter on work. R. Tyson Smith's perspective on masculinity and violence, and his own interest in why men fight, taught me quite a bit about the sociology of gender. And Niobe Way's brilliant work with adolescents, along with our many conversations about "good" and "bad" men, finally gave me a language for the "shadow" I'd spent years attempting to name.

ACKNOWLEDGMENT

Additional thanks to people I spoke to for chapters I didn't ultimately include in the book, but who contributed to this book, and gave me a lot to think about, nonetheless: Tiffany Apcynski, Marcie Bianco, June Carbone, Mike Castle, Anna Marie Clifton, Joelle Emerson, Abby Ferber, Ellen Healy, Caroline Heldman, Aaron Hess, Dacher Keltner, C.J. Pascoe, Andrew Reiner, Tagart Cain Sobotka, Sabastian Caine Roy, Neo L. Sandja, Beth Scheer, Dawn Sharifan, Maxine Williams, and the team at Here Be Dragons. Special thanks to Gaines Blasdel and Cordelia Fine.

I am lucky to have friends who were patient enough to entertain hours of conversation about the world of this book, especially Rae Tutera, Carmel Lobello, and Emily Molina. I am grateful always to Michelle Tea, who is a national treasure. I am indebted to many writers who have supported my work, especially Ann Friedman, Roxane Gay, Garth Greenwell, Saeed Jones, and Liz Plank.

I am grateful for the cover of this book, designed by Xavier Schipani, an incredible talent who I am lucky to also call a friend.

Infinite thanks to my excellent editor at Scribner, Sally Howe, whose faith and sharp vision got me through my hardest moments, and who always (as my mom would say) kept things in perspective. Thanks also to the entire team at Scribner who have worked so hard on behalf of this book; as well as all the lovely and tenacious crew at my publisher across the pond, Canongate.

Thanks to my formidable and brilliant agent, Lindsay Edgecombe, for her excellent guidance on this project, and whose fierce and abiding faith taught me a lot about fighting too.

I am grateful to Chris Lewarne, Andrew Myerson, and Julie Anne Kelly at Haymakers for Hope for welcoming me into their wild and beautiful world. Thanks to Stephen Cash and all the fighters I trained with, for showing me a new way to love and be loved.

I owe much to my coach, Danny Mangual, for teaching me how to come forward, and for believing in me when I didn't believe in myself. Thanks, especially, for being the friend I didn't know how much I needed.

Thank you to my small but mighty family. My sister, Clare, her husband, Dan, my brother, Brett, his wife, Cristina, and my nephews, Ronin and Sebastian. Special thanks to Clare and Brett for sharing their own journeys so candidly, and for always having my back. Brett, I hope to someday be half as good a father as you are. Clare, thank you for showing me how, and why, to fight. You have always been the wisest person I know.

I am so grateful for my mom, for teaching me to see

ACKNOWLEDGMENT

everything, even gender, with a beginner's mind. Her golden core shines on and on.

And thank you to my wife, Jessica Bloom, for showing me the adventure in everything, especially the hard parts, and for being a brave and honest collaborator in life and art. Let's never stop.

Further Reading

These were the most useful works I read as I wrote my own. Without these writers, this book would not exist.

June Carbone, *Marriage Markets: How Inequality Is Remaking the American Family*

Cordelia Fine, *Delusions of Gender*

Allyson Hobbs, *A Chosen Exile: A History of Racial Passing in American Life*

Dacher Keltner, *The Power Paradox: How We Gain and Lose Influence*

Michael Kimmel, *Angry White Men: American Masculinity at the End of an Era*

Nell Irvin Painter, *The History of White People*

C.J. Pascoe, *Dude, You're a Fag: Masculinity and Sexuality in High School*

Robert Sapolsky, *Behave: The Biology of Humans at Our Best and Worst*

R. Tyson Smith, *Fighting for Recognition: Identity, Masculinity, and the Act of Violence in Professional Wrestling*

Niobe Way, *Deep Secrets: Boys' Friendships and the Crisis of Connection*

And:

Bill Buford, *Among the Thugs*

Raewyn Connell, *Masculinities*

James Gilligan, *Violence: Reflections on a National Epidemic*

bell hooks, *The Will to Change: Men, Masculinity, and Love*

Rebecca Solnit, *Men Explain Things to Me*

Shunryu Suzuki, *Zen Mind, Beginner's Mind*

I've read too many excellent articles in print and online to list here, but I especially recommend (and I'm particularly indebted to) the work and thinking of Susan Chira, Lindy West, and Amanda Hess at the *New York Times*; Ta-Nehisi Coates at *The Atlantic*; Ann Friedman and Roxane Gay across many publications; and Saeed Jones at *BuzzFeed* and beyond.

About the Author

Thomas Page McBee was the first transgender man to ever box in Madison Square Garden. He is the author of an award-winning memoir, *Man Alive: A True Story of Violence, Forgiveness and Becoming a Man,* which was named a best book of 2014 by NPR Books, *Buzz-Feed, Kirkus Reviews,* and *Publishers Weekly.* His essays and reportage have appeared in the *New York Times, Playboy, The Atlantic, The Rumpus, Pacific Standard, Glamour,* and *Quartz.* He has given talks on rethinking masculinity to colleges and organizations around the country. He lives with his wife in Brooklyn and Los Angeles.